Taromancy

Predict Your Future

Gerald Boak

Copyright © 2012 Gerald Boak
ISBN 978-1-906958-33-6
New edition 2012

All rights reserved. No part of this work may be reproduced or utilized in any form by any means, electronic or mechanical, including *xerography, photocopying, microfilm,* and *recording,* or by any information storage system without permission in writing from the publishers.

Published by
Mandrake of Oxford
PO Box 250
OXFORD
OX1 1AP (UK)

Contents

1	Author's Note	7
1	A Background to the Oracles	9
2	From I Ching to Taromancy	10
3	The Tree of Life	14
4	How to Select an Oracle	23
5	The First Method of Selecting an Oracle	25
6	The Second Method	27

The Oracles

3 in 1	Leadership	31
4 in 2	Helping Hands	33
5 in 3	Discord	35
6 in 4	Consolidation	37
7 in 5	Union	39
8 in 6	The Silent Flower	41
9 in 7	End of Decrease	43
3 in 8	Stillness	45
4 in 9	United Effort	47
5 in 10	Unrelenting Steps	49
6 in 11	New Life	51
7 in 12	Hidden Deeps	53
8 in 1	Haste	55
9 in 2	Bolder Steps	57
3 in 3	Firm Foundations	59
4 in 4	Pleasure	61
5 in 5	Turmoil	63
6 in 6	The Open Door	65
7 in 7	Cutting Through	67
8 in 8	Assessment	69
9 in 9	The Rainbow	71
3 in 10	Fortunate Days	73
4 in 11	Abundance	75
5 in 12	The Alley	77

6 in 1	Improvements	79
7 in 2	Devotion	81
8 in 3	Necessary Duty	83
9 in 4	Stealth	85
3 in 5	Beyond Reach	87
4 in 6	True Authority	89
5 in 7	Willing Acceptance	91
6 in 8	Respite	93
7 in 9	The Cauldron	95
8 in 10	Begin the Ascent	97
9 in 11	No Reward	99
3 in 12	Jackals	101
4 in 1	Careful Husbandry	103
5 in 2	Two Friends	105
6 in 3	New Ground	107
7 in 4	Remain Loyal	109
8 in 5	Shut and Open	111
9 in 6	The Glow	113
3 in 7	Reunion	115
4 in 8	Cutting Down	117
5 in 9	The Servant	119
6 in 10	Spring	121
7 in 11	Filling a Jug	123
8 in 12	Brother and Sister	125
9 in 1	The New Road	127
3 in 2	The Abyss	129
4 in 3	The First Gifts	131
5 in 4	Providence	133
6 in 5	Marriage	135
7 in 6	The Pendulum	137
8 in 7	Weighing Memories	139
9 in 8	Making Entry	141
3 in 9	Water and Rock	143
4 in 10	Denial	145
5 in 11	The Cart	147
6 in 12	The Roadside	149
7 in 1	Bounds of Reason	151

8 in 2	Management	153
9 in 3	Beginning and Preparing	155
3 in 4	Unassailable	157
4 in 5	Unbreakable	159
5 in 6	The Storm	161
6 in 7	The Confident Voice	163
7 in 8	The Iron Grip	165
8 in 9	The Hinge	167
9 in 10	Integrity	169
3 in 11	The Friendly Voice	171
4 in 12	The Net	173
5 in 1	Expertise	175
6 in 2	The Important Rose	177
7 in 3	Two Trees	179
8 in 4	Contingency	181
9 in 5	The Dwarf and the Giant	183
3 in 6	The Owl	185
4 in 7	Square and Circle	187
5 in 8	Talent and Aptitude	189
6 in 9	Eagle and Lion	191
7 in 10	The Carver	193
8 in 11	Responding to Necessity	195
9 in 12	The Shadows	197

Appendix 1:
Meaning of Numbers in the Series 1-12
Star Signs and Tarot Cards 199

Meaning of Numbers in the Series 3 – 9 204
The Planets

List of Oracles 208

Author's Note

The 84 oracles were first published in 1985. They were intended for the experienced hand at divination, and have remained in widespread demand ever since. I hope this fully revised edition, which contains the same oracles but in less technical language, will appeal to those only now setting out to explore fortune telling. After a quarter of a century in use, I believe their following justifies this major revision

Apart from their plainer style, a new Summary and in-depth Conclusion now accompanies each oracle. These replace the earlier and limited Notes, and explain even the smallest areas of interest. Together with extra and helpful background material in the first three chapters, I believe these sizeable additions will provide a more complete and user-friendly tool of divination.

Finally, and on a purely technical note, the astrological aspects behind the oracles agree with the work of Aleister Crowley in his dictionary of correspondences, Liber 777 vel Prolegomena Symbolica ad Systemam (etc.) published privately in 1909 and adopted since as a standard work of reference. Two of those correspondences were amended in his 1944 edition of *The Book of Thoth*. In that book Crowley made a fundamental error in his Key Scale of the tables, incorrectly assigning Aries to Tarot trump XVII and Aquarius to trump IV, whereas, and by his own admission, they should be counterchanged. Fearing more hawk-eyed diviners will question my choice of attributions, I thought it safest to explain in advance.

GB
Valencia, 2009

Part 1

1
A Background to the Oracles

By far the best-known book of oracles is the *I Ching*, or *Book of Changes*. This ancient Chinese classic is one of the most important books in the world's literature. It has influenced statecraft, shaped philosophies, inspired sages and captured the imagination of people worldwide. This begs the question: With a leading guide already available, is there any need for another book of oracles?

The *I Ching* enjoys an unrivaled status, and any relative newcomer must stand in the dock and defend itself. The reader needs to feel confident that the book stems from a reputable source, and has not simply been plucked from thin air. By revealing how the 84 oracles developed, and why their driving force has a recognised pedigree, it will also become clear why there is a need for the present alternative. This background will not only help to reach an understanding of how oracles work, but contribute to better results from the all-important divination process. Having the right tools of the trade is only half the battle; the other half is knowing why they choose to behave in the way they do. It will take only a little time to cover this ground, which is central nonetheless and advisable if we are to remove any lingering doubts.

From I Ching to Taromancy

The *I Ching*'s basic formulation is attributed to Fu-hsi, the legendary Chinese ruler of 3322 B.C. His contribution began as eight strange trigrams. They were patterns of three straight lines placed one above the other, with each line either whole (--) or having a short division (- -) in the centre. No two trigrams were the same. With their interplay of whole or divided lines, they symbolized the trinity of heaven above, earth below and humanity in between. Their various designs were seen to portray the unfolding cycle of life's profound mysteries; the changing seasons, the rise and fall of all created things. At this early stage in its evolution, the *I Ching* had yet to flower as a written book. Even so, by word of mouth the trigrams gained a respectful following, quickly spreading from the royal court to the outside world.

It is not clear in which century the trigrams were expanded by placing them on top of each other, but this logical development produced 64 unique patterns of six lines called hexagrams. What is known is that some time around 1143 B.C., King Wan, founder of the Kau dynasty, added his text to those hexagrams. This step came to form the heart of the *I Ching* as it now stands. From then on, the hexagrams were regarded as a book of oracles with magical powers, illustrating the eternal shifts and changes of universal tides. Over the following years hundreds of scholars contributed to the book's Appendixes, until the first complete imperial edition was published in 1715 – more than 5,000 years after Fu-hsi. Anyone wishing to divine the future had only to cast a handful of yarrow stalks a number of times, and the way they fell would indicate a specific oracle to provide the answer. That oracle would have a general significance, a kind of over-view, which in turn was clarified by details of the hidden meaning behind each of the six lines. Simple, thorough and unquestionably effective. Or at least, it was unquestionable in its day.

Few people have ever doubted the vision of the *I Ching*. It is an incomparable masterpiece. Sadly it is also (and unavoidably) a monument to its age, brimming with mystical concepts completely alien to the contemporary world. Numerous attempts have been made to update the text, so lending the book a more modern and universal appeal, but that is rather like trying to put a glove on a foot – it was never intended to serve that purpose. What was instantly meaningful to the people of ancient China will never readily translate into modern Western terms, at least, not without destroying most of the underlying wisdom that set the book apart in the first place. One core problem is that the early written Chinese characters were not words as we understand them, but symbols of the writer's ideas. One pioneering translator had to admit that after spending years writing a direct translation, he came to realise that through the confusing nature of the original text he had completely missed the point.[1]

Exalted though the book may be, for many Westerners today it reflects a culture and era too remote to comprehend. As a time capsule it is without equal, yet it is hard to feel comfortable with oracles that advise; 'Remove your toes. Friends will come, between you and whom there will be mutual confidence.' They are almost impossible to digest, regardless of the interpreter's skills. For all these reasons the *I Ching* is a book of divination only for those willing to accept a pale modern version, in which case they too will invariably miss the original point;

---

1 James Legge. He reached this conclusion in 1874, twenty years after his hand-written manuscript had been accidentally soaked for over a month in water of the Red Sea. By careful manipulation it was fully restored, but found to be "of no service at all" when the real clue to the book finally came to him.

or else they must be prepared to enter into the spirit of the book, and study the academic work of sinologists who translated the original texts, but who in turn were loathe to explain the folklore and images conveyed by those texts. If these alternatives are too much to consider, anyone who needs a quick and simple way to predict the future will find their options strictly limited.

A need to foretell the direction of our lives has been with us since the beginning of recorded history. It is a need so consuming and powerful as to be almost instinctive. In desperate times, and for understandable reasons, that need is significantly heightened. Ours is a high-speed, no-nonsense and harshly realistic culture, yet to fill a void in our lives the daily horoscope is one of the most sought-out items in any newspaper. But the daily horoscope is a generalized view; correct for some, wildly adrift for others. The remaining alternative is to visit a professional fortune-teller, although this can prove an expensive contribution to the pocket of a charlatan. Obviously it would be better to divine the future for ourselves, using a technique that delivers trustworthy results.

Tarot cards and astrology are the mainstays of fortune-telling in the West. The downside is, they come at a price most people are unwilling to pay. The main drawback of either system is that to reach a level of competence can take years of application. The student soon learns that intuition plays a major role, far exceeding the dry meaning of a card or planetary aspect. Intuition must be nurtured and refined. In the early stages of learning, failures are inevitable and often deliver a quite undeserved blow to self-confidence. It simply takes time. Reliable predictions are achieved by those determined enough to stay the grim course of practice, study and more practice, which is where most people lose interest. On the other hand, Tarot cards and astrology do have a major advantage. Although of ancient origins, they share the ability to speak to us in a language we understand; they are part of our roots, our own history and cultural heritage. Their meanings may be hidden beneath curious symbols, but once they are understood everything eventually falls into place. The trick is to unravel those meanings when they combine in unexpected ways, perhaps to tell a complicated story. At other times we may need to detect when they do not answer our question at all, but are revealing the causes of a long-standing and contributory problem, and are helpfully suggesting a cure. In true divination, we sometimes find the answer we need most is one relating to a question we did not think to ask.

With all these points in mind, it was evident that what was needed was a manual as quick and simple to employ as the *I Ching,* but having none of its obvious shortcomings. What was needed was a collection of oracles prepared specifically for the West.

This, then, is why the precursor of the present book came into being, but not before a significant problem had been resolved. It was recognised from the outset that the oracles would need a firm base in tradition. Without respected principles to support them, the oracles would lack a true voice. They could lay no claim to authenticity and they would almost certainly fail in practice.

The solution was found in a cornerstone of the Western mystery tradition, in an intriguing symbol known as the Tree of Life.

2
The Tree of Life

In Genesis (3.22) the Bible says, 'And the Lord God said, Behold, the man is become as one of us, to know good and evil; and now, lest he put forth his hand, and take also of the Tree of Life[1] and eat, and live for ever:' – from which point on the next verse reveals how Adam was banished from Eden, to prevent him from touching the Tree. Enough damage had been done: thanks to the Serpent, he had already acquired the divine right of identifying good and evil. In 3.24 the text continues; 'So he drove out the man; and he placed at the east of the garden of Eden Cherubims, and a flaming sword which turned every way, to keep the way of the Tree of Life.'[2] Even in the Bible, the Tree was recognised as a powerful and potentially dangerous entity, leading as it did to the prospect of eternal life.

Hebrews were not the first or only race to make mention of the Tree. It surfaces in ancient Egypt, Assyria, India, Germany and China to name only a few countries where early accounts or images have survived. In short, it may be considered a universal concept, adopted as a symbol in our struggle to understand the meaning of life and the mystery of Creation.

---

1 My capitals.
2 Ditto.

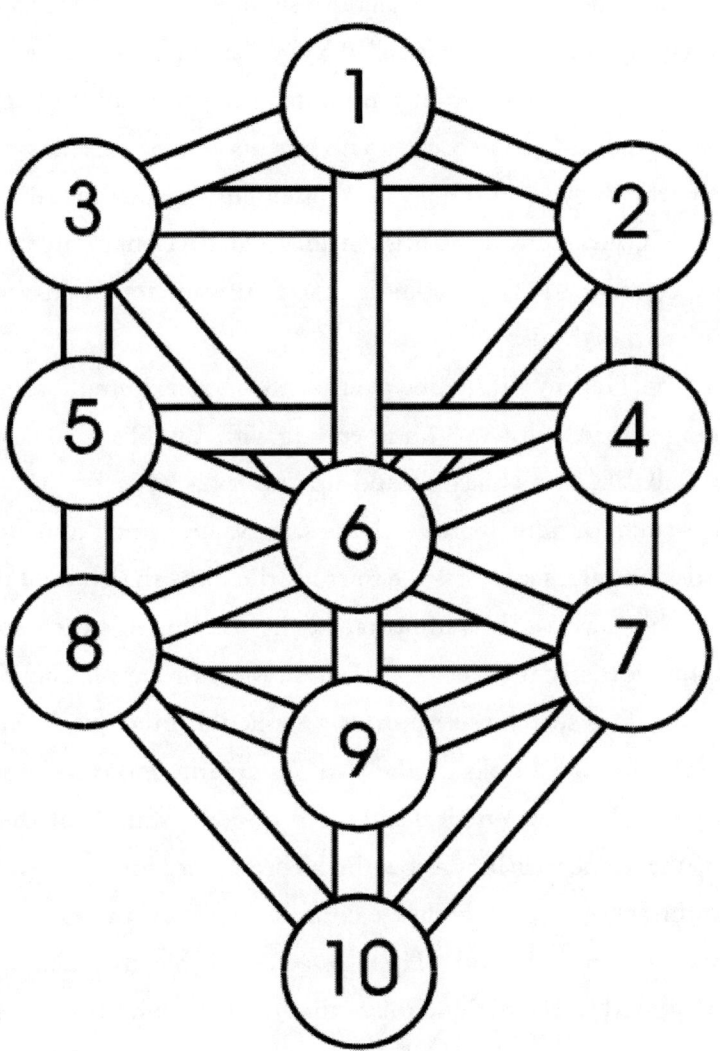

As might be expected, not all representations of the Tree are the same. In Norse mythology it is called Yggdrasil, and depicted as a lush tree sprouting from the top of a mountain. In other lands the image is more stylized and geometric, with no hint about it of organic growth. This is particularly so in the mystical discipline of Judaism known as the Qabalah, which through Christian links added weight to the western mystery tradition. It is a tradition that flourishes to this day as an alternative to orthodox religion.

In the Hebrew alphabet every letter has a numerical value, beginning with Aleph (A) =1 and ending with Tau (T) = 400. In the Judaic Qabalah, this ability to add up the total value of any word allows a search for other words with the same value. From this matching of words and values it is possible to study the ideas shared but hidden between those words. It is important to realise that it is the concept *behind* the words that receives the attention, not simply the words themselves. This search was rigorously applied throughout the sacred Torah (the first five books of the Old Testament) and other notable holy texts in Hebrew. A typical and often-quoted example of the sort of thing that came to light was that the Hebrew word for unity (AChD), used in the sense of perfect divine completeness, has the value of 13, whereas the name of God (IHVH or Jehovah) has the value of 26. This suggested to the early scholars that the God who thundered to their prophets was a direct reflection or extension of unity, for 13 plus 13 equals 26. As this is nowhere mentioned in the Torah, it is not too difficult to see how new streams of religious thought could spring from the revelations of the Qabalah.

The idea of unity apparently dividing into two is the starting point for the Qabalistic Tree of Life. This is a symbol, a drawing, a description on paper of a chain of cause and effect. It is not a reality, in the sense that it might be found somewhere like a hidden and marvellous growth. It is an attempt by those who studied the Qabalah in ages past to describe how everything in existence sprang from a common source. A modern physicist would describe the source at that moment in time as the Big Bang, but that was something unknown when the Tree was depicted.

According to the Tree of Life, before unity existed there was something called Ain Soph Aur, 'the limitless light', which in three stages condensed into a realm of creative potential. (This seems to describe the Big Bang fairly accurately, which leads us to wonder at the perception of those early scholars). From that far-flung potential there condensed the first stage of Creation; unity, which some see as God and others see in terms of pure energy.

Unity was now existing and whole, but without any physical properties. When unity became aware of its existence, rather like (to use a crude analogy) someone catching a glimpse of themselves in an extraordinary dream, unity had acquired conscious awareness. So was born the second and conscious stage of Creation. This cascade of action and reaction, cause and effect, trickled down through a total of ten stages until, at the tenth stage, it came to a halt as physical matter. The world and universe we know were complete, as was the principle of the Tree of Life.

The ten stages are shown on the Tree as spheres, arranged in an elegant pattern and connected by a network of 22 paths (see illustration). The spheres represent specific states; they are a description of what Creation had achieved up to that point, whereas the connecting paths describe the process of change between one sphere and the next. In this sense the paths are routes of humming activity, whereas the spheres are static and unchanging. If this arrangement sounds rather absurd, think of the Tree as a computer circuit board. On any circuit board there are various electronic components, soldered into place. They cannot move, and internally they always behave in the same way. Connecting those components are inlaid paths, along which rushes the electric current. Every time the current passes through a fixed component, the current is transformed; it pulses in a different way. All this is started by pressing a button, and it ends as something visible on a screen. The Tree of Life is almost exactly like that; a circuit of rushing energy, which is transformed by every fixed component it encounters and initiated by the topmost button.

The Tree of Life launched many new schools of thought, inspired in the main by one of the most ancient books of the Qabalah, the *Sepher Yetzirah*, or Book of Formation. Scholars, holy men and sorcerers alike poured over the symbol, seeing in the spheres and paths new ways to explain nature. Many of them wondered if it might be possible to climb back up the Tree, in a manner of speaking, and so reach dizzying heights of spirituality. The answer was yes, in their minds they could, and many secret societies and brotherhoods spent their lives training to do just that. This was a road fraught with danger, for the mind is a complex and delicate affair. As some students found to their cost, one slip and the result could be madness – or worse. It was a case of the higher you went, the harder you fell.

On the brighter side, the 22 paths were attractive to Qabalists, who with their love of numbers and symbols found they could allocate to each path all manner of plants, perfumes, animals, astrological signs and gemstones, etc, which through their associated symbolism or inherent qualities tied in nicely with the nature of that particular path. Of prime importance were the 22 mysterious characters of the Hebrew alphabet; they shared paths with streams of divine emanations bearing such grand names as Scintillating Intelligence, or the Triumphal One. Over time the Tree of Life became a vast repository, in which everything in existence had a fitting place. Even Tarot cards.

The most important cards in the Tarot are the 22 trumps, sometimes known as Major Arcana or greater secrets. These are picture cards, with enigmatic scenes that are at once baffling and hauntingly familiar. Where and when the Tarot originated, we do not know. Theories abound, but they remain theories. What is almost certain is that the playing cards we use today are derived from the lesser secrets, or four suits, that accompany the trumps. In the 19th century it was recognised by a leading magical Order, called the Hermetic Order of the Golden Dawn, that there might be a link between the 22 trump cards and the 22 paths of the Tree of Life. After some detailed research, which included the study of rare and precious manuscripts in museum libraries, the link was proven. The symbolism behind each card could be matched with a corresponding path on the Tree: there was a trump card of the Tarot to fit every path. But the new development did not stop there. Long before that, the signs of the zodiac had been allocated to 12 paths that were their natural home. When the 22 trump cards were placed on the paths, 12 of those cards were seen to share an identity with individual star signs. It was a major turning point for the future of divination.

The Tree of Life is a dynamic symbol. Not only does it describe the stages of Creation, it can be applied to any act or situation, great or small, that has a beginning and end. Should you fancy a cup of tea, then from 'fancy' to 'drink' can have its own Tree. Cradle to the grave, marriage to divorce, rags to riches and back again; everything conceivable has a course, a route of action and reaction that can be explained, like a universe in miniature. This is one reason why it has such a strong following in the mystery schools; almost like a map, it is possible to take any situation or event and plot its most likely course, with the added bonus of being able to detect in advance if matters are in the right place, or badly out of line. It is beyond question one of the most potent and vibrant symbols in existence. None of this can be appreciated by a glance at its design; it is something which is only understood following a study of what it really says. Hence the need for mystery schools, occult lodges, magical Orders and the like.

From this discovery by the Golden Dawn, it was possible to describe a planet moving into a star sign by using a voice other than that of astrology – that of the Tarot. The Tarot images and characters, active in their unique way, would react according to the nature of the forces represented by that planet. Mars, for instance, once regarded as the god of war, would bring turmoil and upheaval; Jupiter, the god who presided over banquets, would bring stability and security. Then we have Mercury, the winged messenger, symbol of communication and trickery; Venus, goddess of love – and so on. All these varying energies would effect the Tarot trump accordingly, and modify the situation represented by that card. (A full list of meanings behind the planets, Tarot trumps and star signs is given in the Appendix. There is, however, no need to commit any of these meanings to memory; the oracles take all those matters into account.)

Just as the paths on the Tree of Life are home to all manner of symbols, so also are the ten spheres. The main symbol for each sphere is a planet, where the nature of the planet was seen to represent the energies (turmoil, communication, love, etc.) exhibited by the sphere. This adds another and unique aspect to divination by the oracles, but first we need to explore how the oracles are made to work.

Through a straightforward process of random selection, the querent (the person asking the question) discovers that a certain planet is moving into a particular star sign and Tarot trump. This process of random selection is equivalent to casting the yarrow stalks of the *I Ching*, or shuffling Tarot cards in preparation for a reading. How can this random process be effective? The famous psychoanalyst C.G.

Jung spent years working on this puzzle, for he was fascinated by the stunning 'coincidences' of accurate results produced by such methods. Jung's theories were described by the author Arthur Koestler in his milestone book, *The Roots of Coincidence*, thus: 'It is painful to watch how a great mind ... gets entangled in its own verbiage'. (Jung had been outlining his bizarre concept of 'non-synchronous synchronicity'.) For an absolute certainty, Jung would have done better to hold up his hands and admit, 'I have no idea.' Nobody does, at least in scientific terms. Even Koestler wisely stopped short of forming conclusions. Nevertheless, it is worth considering that the *I Ching* has survived for thousands of years, and nothing dominates that long if it is fundamentally useless or flawed. While the Tarot is a mere youngster in comparison, close to a thousand years of use has not seen its popularity diminish; if anything it has increased.

When the oracles speak of a planet entering a star sign, neither will relate to their actual position in the heavens. Like the whole or divided lines of the I Ching they are purely symbols, employed to represent a type of force currently in motion. Some planets will be comfortably associated with the chosen star sign and corresponding trump; others will immediately shriek of interference and discord. The oracle will reflect these matches or mismatches as part of its judgement of the situation.

Finally, the greater part of that judgement will depend on issues connected with the planet other than its astrological associations. As mentioned above, the ten spheres on the Tree of Life each have a planet assigned to them, according to their harmonious natures. What the oracles take into account is how close, or how far apart, that sphere and planet is positioned on the Tree in relation to the path of the star sign and Tarot trump. Sometimes they will be in comfortable agreement and show upward progress; at other times they may be so unbalanced or opposed that the oracle will flash a direct warning.

How the 'thumbs up' or 'thumbs down' replies are delivered, depends largely on the character portrayed by the trump.

His or her reaction, his or her plain sailing or struggles, gains or losses, are described in terms appropriate to that character. We see the affairs of 'the emperor', as he controls his empire with greater or lesser success; or 'the hermit', as his plans go forward to reach an ideal conclusion, or crumble into dust. These episodes form the main substance of the oracle: it is a concise passage which illustrates how the character's progress is shaped by the forces at work. The accompanying notes that guide us through those forces and changes, plus further details of the oracles themselves, are described in the closing pages of the next chapter. There we will learn how to select an oracle in answer to a question, and what we will find when we turn to that oracle's page.

3
How to Select an Oracle

There are two ways to proceed with the divination, and the choice of either is solely a matter of personal preference. The key is to try both, and see which method works best for you. Yet before starting out, we need to consider the attitude necessary for a successful divination, and what prior thought should be given to the question itself.

It may be stating the obvious, but it is as well to underscore the fact: divination should never be undertaken lightly, as in a party trick. Once it is known at any gathering that a way to tell fortunes is on hand, everyone wants to take part. That is not to say divination cannot be arranged for several people at one sitting, taking each person in turn. What must be appreciated is that divination is a serious matter. We do not understand why it works, any more than a scientist can explain the secrets of time. Quite ordinary people can have sudden premonitions that prove to be entirely accurate, and sometimes life-saving. Ask any scientist how this happens, and that scientist will merely shrug. At best, you will hear 'just a coincidence' offered somewhere in a string of possible theories. A lack of explanation changes nothing. With the correct approach, divination can produce a highly meaningful result.

Basically, it comes down to common sense. A flippant or light-hearted attitude will produce nothing of value – apart, possibly, from a slap on the wrist in the oracle's reply. A question put with sincerity, and with the intention of receiving a truthful answer, will always provide the best results. A suitable atmosphere contributes enormously. There is everything to be gained by burning incense, sitting quietly in meditation and lighting candles if it helps to set the mood. Better that, than being surrounded by clinking glasses, loud music and garrulous voices. Whatever it takes to settle you in a sincere and respectful frame of mind – that is what should be done, and know that you could do no more. Effort and sincerity, integrity and a calm atmosphere untroubled by distractions; these are conditions everyone should aim for.

The question itself, and how it is phrased, can in turn be a surprising minefield

'Should I move to Rome, or Paris?' An important question for a lucky individual somewhere no doubt; but impossible for any oracle to answer. No worthy oracle in existence will ever come up with advice along the lines of, 'Move to Rome.' There is only one way to approach the problem of choosing between alternatives. The question has to be put twice: 'Would a move to Rome be fortunate for me?', and the oracle's advice should be noted. Then put the same question again, but this time replacing Rome with Paris. Once the two answers are compared, then an informed decision can be made. Obviously, the most favourable response is the one to consider.

Similarly with forms of ambiguity. Vagueness must be avoided. The story is told of a great military leader, who before taking his troops into a decisive battle sought the advice of a reliable seeress. He asked her if he took on this battle, would there be victory? Yes, was her reply. Emboldened with confidence, off he went to war – and lost. Later, and with considerable umbrage, he confronted the seeress and asked how she could have got it so wrong. She explained that she had not. Through his self-centered attitude, he had not thought to ask which side would enjoy the victory...

Apocryphal tales apart, the moral holds true. In any question be specific as to people, times, places, or any other relevant factor that could be misconstrued. Getting it wrong can be a serious mistake.

The First Method of Selecting an Oracle

Take a complete suit from a deck of ordinary playing cards, choosing whichever suit you prefer. You will need only 12 cards from this suit, so discard the king. Now you will have cards with a value from 1 to 10, plus the jack and the queen. For our purposes, the jack will count as 11 and the queen as 12.

Place the cards face down on a flat surface, and while thinking hard of your question, shuffle them around as you would dominos. (Professional gamblers will tell you that this is the only way to shuffle cards by hand with a guaranteed random outcome.) Stop shuffling when ready.

Gather up the cards and place them in a stack, still face down.

Remove the top three cards. Turn the fourth card over and write down its number.

Now turn all the cards face up. Remove those numbered 1, 2, 10, 11 and 12, and put them away to one side.

Proceed as before; turn over the seven remaining cards, and concentrate on the question while shuffling. When ready, put the cards in a stack face down, remove the top three cards and turn over the fourth. This provides the second number you need and completes the selection process.

The first number you obtained will range between 1 and 12. For the purpose of this example, we will imagine it was the number 11. The second number you obtained will range between 3 and 9, and here we can imagine it was the number 8. To find which oracle answers your question, you must write the two numbers down in the *reverse* order to which they were obtained, and in our example it would be written as; 8 in 11.

The first number obtained (11) points to the star sign and Tarot trump. Between them they show the background to the enquiry, the stage on which the Tarot characters will perform. This background has to be established first; without knowing where in the field of human interest they are supposed to be looking, the oracles cannot perform with any reliability. Then along comes a moving force, sometimes beneficial, sometimes not, but either way this force will make its entrance, pushing in, working in, acting in our lives. This moving force is the second number (8), representing the intruding planet, and as it acts *in* our lives, it must be written in the sequence that indicates this effect: 8 in 11. (This is equivalent to an astrologer talking in terms of Jupiter in Virgo, Mars in Leo, Venus in Scorpio, etc.)

By referring to the List of Oracles at the beginning of this book, you will see that 8 in 11 is the oracle 'Responding to Necessity', on *page* — , where at the top of the page 8 is shown to represent the planet Mercury, and 11 represents the star sign of Aquarius with Tarot trump XVII, The Star.

The Second Method

All you will need for this method is a coin and a single dice. (Strictly speaking a single dice is called a die, but the word is rarely used.) Do please remember to keep your question firmly in mind at the beginning of each of the three steps described below.

Step One. Throw the dice. Note whether the score is even (2, 4 or 6) or odd (1, 3, or 5) but make no further use of the number. At this stage we need only to learn if the next step will be even or odd.

Step Two. If the first step was even, throw the dice twice and add together the two scores. If the first step was odd, throw the dice once and note the score. In either case the number obtained at the end of this stage will be between 1 and 12.

Step Three. Throw the dice once again and note the score. Take the coin. With heads counting as two and tails counting as three, toss the coin and add the resulting score to that of the dice just thrown. This will yield a number in total between 3 and 9, and completes the selection process.

If we assume that Step Two gave us the number 7, and Step Three gave us the number 6, the two numbers must be written down in reverse order as, 6 in 7. This follows the same practice as that described in the First Method of Selecting an Oracle. By turning to the List of Oracles, we see that 6 in 7 refers to the oracle 'The Confident Voice' on *page* —, where 6 is shown to be the Sun, and 7 is the star sign of Libra with Tarot trump VIII, Adjustment.

The planet, star sign and Tarot trump details are given solely to furnish a background interest. They are a way of explaining from the start the forces at work, although the main point of interest, of course, will be the oracle itself. As mentioned briefly in the previous chapter, this takes the form of a concise and descriptive passage. To reiterate; it is an account of how the Tarot characters respond to the forces at work. Some characters will react favourably to Saturn, for example, while others will be severely hindered and find themselves in difficulty. It must never be forgotten that these characters are not 'someone imaginary' or 'someone else': whether there is mention of the emperor, the hermit, the lovers or any other of the twelve trumps, they are images of the situation or person to whom the question relates. Having said that, in many instances the oracles do describe scenes where there are no principal characters. The combination of planet and trump renders it almost impossible to reveal future trends by portraying the actions of people; the outcome is better expressed by images of deep rivers and other similar metaphors. In these cases the meaning is grasped more easily by an evocative passage describing moods and settings, for example, rather than actions. Whichever route the oracle takes, it should be allowed to conjure in the mind a personal connection, a link with private circumstances. See the events described as reflecting family or social situations; imagine other details mentioned in the oracle – for example, where it may warn of prowling jackals – as symbols of real and possibly already known threats, skulking around, waiting their moment to pounce. It hardly matters that all these images will be explained by the accompanying Summary and Conclusion. What counts is that they speak directly to the recipient of the message. Every divination is a personal matter; only the individual concerned can judge for themselves what the oracle really means for them in their private affairs.

After the oracle is the Summary. This expands on the oracle's meaning, and explains why it has adopted its particular tone and opinion. Armed with this information, it is then much easier to follow up a negative response with a second question, which takes into account the warnings received. By a process of elimination, or by avoiding the stated pitfalls and errors, it might still be possible to achieve a satisfactory direction and outcome.

Following the Summary is a Conclusion. This is a way of wrapping up everything said previously, so that no area of doubt can remain. It is the 'bottom line', the final closure to the question. It is here that the astrological effects are explained in more detail, and how these might be modified by their relation to the Tree of Life. There is no technical or esoteric terminology involved in either the Summary or the Conclusion. The intention has been to sweep away all such confusion and keep to a language everyone can understand. It is sincerely hoped that this fresh approach will take divination out of the hands of specialists, and put it where it belongs: in the hands of people who will enjoy the opportunity to glimpse other worlds, and find personal satisfaction in predicting the future for themselves.

Part 2
The Oracles

3 in 1

3=Saturn, 1=the star sign Aries and Tarot trump IV, The Emperor. Saturn rules the element water, Aries is of fire.

Leadership

The young emperor has matured into adulthood. Calmness and consideration now shape his decisions. His maturity brings improvement to the empire.

Youthful inexperience has no place in leadership. A land with great promise demands a guide with clear vision. Lacking maturity, the emperor dallied with trifles. Beyond the walls of his palace the land approached ruin.

Maturity of mind is not a product of years. Time is an empty passage. How we fill that passage is a measure of the echo of our steps.

The mature emperor knows his strengths and he admits to his weaknesses. Facing them is his greatest achievement. In this way he fulfills the obligations of leadership.

Past errors will not resurface.

Summary

The emperor can be an individual of either sex or a collective of any number of people. In either case the emperor brings an influence to bear on those around him. In the past he was indecisive or given to rash decisions with little concern for reality. This had a damaging effect; it restricted progress by not capitalizing on opportunities as and when they appeared. His change of mind has little to do with age; it is more an internal awareness that he needs to change. He is now aware of his strong and weak points; facing up to them gains him trust and respect. It is, perhaps, the awareness that not all things are possible, but by starting afresh and concentrating on what can be achieved there is less room for disappointment. He has learned a valuable lesson.

Conclusion

Saturn in Aries indicates the imposition of controls on others. The star sign's associated Tarot card, trump IV, The Emperor, means conquest, vigour, rashness and ambition. This compares well with the fiery nature of Aries. In both sign and trump the fire is a blustering flame, as yet fierce and lacking refinement. Saturn, on the other hand, occupies a high position on the Tree of Life and commands respect. The forces it represents can slow matters down or bring them to a halt; but they can also produce an understanding of life's complexities. They can create order, where there was disorder and confusion. Only these positive forces will apply in the case of the Tarot character; it is too strong to bow to complete restriction. It is the waters of Saturn serving to calm the stormy fire of Aries.

4 in 2

4= Jupiter, 2 = the star sign of Taurus and Tarot trump V, The Hierophant. Jupiter rules the element water, Taurus is of earth.

Helping Hands

A new tower is rising on the landscape. Brick by brick, stone by stone, the foundations are being laid. They are broad and strong.

Help will arrive to complete the tower. People are drawn to strength and stability, to the security of permanence. Promising beginnings attract encouragement. The young and talented will gain support, the fresh and innovative will find open doorways. Where there is promise there are helping hands.

When complete a tower will serve many uses. From raised heights events are seen at a distance; within its solid walls people are safe.

Brick by brick, stone by stone, the tower will justify helping hands.

Summary

The tower is an image of achievement. The broad and strong foundations mean that events proceed from a sound proposition. In most cases a workable plan or a sensible ambition wins backing from people in a position to help; the better the proposition, the more likely the offers of support and encouragement. When the end is reached 'events are seen at a distance'; this means that widened horizons allow more opportunities to be assessed, and potential difficulties spotted before they can develop too far. The final result is so gratifying that those who gave their support will feel rewarded by their contribution.

Conclusion

Jupiter in Taurus indicates the desire to expand resources and improve material circumstances. The star sign's corresponding Tarot card, trump V, The Hierophant, means stubborn strength, toil, wise counsel. The character is depicted by the oracle as a tower of strength. On the Tree of Life the sign and trump occupy an advanced path between the spheres of Jupiter and Neptune, called Mercy and Wisdom respectively. The entrance of Jupiter into the world of the trump is a clear signal that everything is in perfect order. By virtue of its location on the Tree, the planet is the correct starting point for the Hierophant's advance. Jupiter is a powerful force and its number, 4, suggests the solidity of a cube, a foundation stone capable of supporting a great weight. Known for its magnificence and bounty, Jupiter will readily attract attention and assistance. The water of Jupiter nurtures and invigorates the quiet earth of Taurus.

5 in 3

5= Mars, 3= the star sign of Gemini and Tarot trump VI, The Lovers. Mars rules the element fire, Gemini is of air.

Discord

In the centre of a thunderstorm, people lower their heads. Joining together in peaceful agreement becomes impossible in the open. Even in sheltered places people remain still. They watch and they listen. A storm above brings the world below to a halt.

Objectives are abandoned in the centre of a thunderstorm. The shared roads of destiny are forced apart. For a time discord reigns.

When the storm is over, people stop and reflect. They ask if the storm was a sign. They wonder if the moment was interrupted for a reason. They question the correctness of joining together. Some will insist that a storm means nothing, and encourage the resumption of a peaceful agreement.

Many people ignore storms. Yet in the centre of a battlefield they will lift their heads, and call out to the heavens for help.

Summary

The thunderstorm is an image of a moment forcefully interrupted. In ordinary affairs this will most likely take the form of a disagreement, a clash of minds or a blunt rejection. A core issue raised by the oracle is whether this should be taken as a sign of mysterious intervention. The truth is that any profound disagreement is a sign that the initial proposal was badly conceived, and to press ahead regardless would be foolish. Experience shows that in almost every case, where there is a trail of infuriating obstacles to a desired goal it is usually best to walk away. How to decide who or what sets up those obstacles, and how they manage to go about it is beyond the capacity of most of us to answer. But the message here is clear enough: there is no advantage in this direction.

Conclusion

Mars in Gemini indicates the tendency to waver indecisively, and to squander time and effort. Gemini's corresponding Tarot card, trump VI, The Lovers, means intelligence, intuition and swift adaptability. These meanings are overturned by the entrance of Mars, the god of war. The last energy the trump needs is one that overheats, disrupts and destroys. On the Tree of Life the sign and trump occupy a high path, well on their way to the lofty realms of spirit. The entry of Mars signals a backward step, introducing an angry imbalance. It is the fire of Mars scorching and dispersing the air of Gemini.

6 in 4

6= Sun, 4= the star sign Cancer and Tarot trump VII, The Chariot. Sun rules the element air, Cancer is of water.

Consolidation

The charioteer must prepare for battle. Forces of opposition are gathering in the distance. Dark clouds span the horizon.

Yet the charioteer should not be dismayed by feelings of alarm. The forces of opposition are distant: they present no immediate threat.

The charioteer should prepare his chariot and steeds with calmness and care. Weapons should be kept near at hand. It is a time for the planning of forward action.

Direct conflict has yet to take place. At this moment the charioteer holds a position of security. He can watch the movements of those in the distance and predict their intentions. There can be no surprise move made against him.

To advance towards the horizon would not be favourable; it would stir unnecessary reaction. Beyond the safeguard of consolidation there are no indications that advance or retreat would be of value.

Summary

The warning here is that matters are out of balance. The 'dark clouds' visible on the horizon suggest that looming problems have not gone unnoticed elsewhere and support may be reducing. The advantage, however, is that any disputes – which may be no more than differences of opinion – are known and their climax is remote for the moment. Also, the objectors cannot move without revealing their intentions.

The advice is not to react now with undue alarm. It is a matter of preparing one's argument (the 'chariot and steeds') and ensuring that one is mentally ready to face any challenges ('Weapons should be kept near at hand'.) Note the emphasis on preparation; there is no call for other action. At the moment do little more than plan and remain watchful.

Conclusion

Sun in Cancer traditionally indicates the acquisition of material resources to provide security, especially in the home. Tarot trump VII, The Chariot, illustrates success through initiative, the surmounting of obstacles and victory through effort. On the Tree of Life the sign and trump occupy the path between Saturn and Mars. In this oracle the intruding planet is Sun, which would normally indicate the appearance of synthesis, balance and harmony. The location of Sun on the Tree, however, points to a step out of line in terms of upward progress for the Tarot character – in fact, it is a retrograde step. The Charioteer represents high intelligence and ability; when someone with these characteristics is seen to make a bad move observers are concerned. Barriers may be raised and doors closed. Under these circumstances one can only make the best of circumstances as they stand. Provided no further steps are taken out of character, the beneficial nature of Sun will ensure no damage will befall this charioteer. It is the air of Sun disturbing ripples on the waters of Cancer.

7 in 5

7=Venus, 5= the star sign Leo, and Tarot trump XI, Lust. Venus rules the element fire, Leo is of fire.

Union

The naked woman sits astride the mighty lion. Progress is made through the union of strength and weakness.

The great wild lion consents to be guided by the naked woman. The apparently weak and the manifestly strong are bound in unconventional union. Those who act with bold inspiration will rise above the limits of convention.

When two opposites approach each other with mutual approval, their union combines in a balanced advantage. A new journey can proceed without resistance. The journey's end brings benefits to both.

When strength supports weakness, and weakness acts as a guide, the two admire in each other a virtue hidden from the lesser crowd.

Summary

The naked woman is a symbol of apparent weakness and vulnerability. The lion, conversely, represents unmistakable strength. This highly unusual pair may represent two people, or one person and their desired goal. The oracle reveals how matters are not always as they seem, and the truth of a situation is often a surprise. The main issue is that two opposites see in each other a virtue not recognised by others. That virtue may take the form of hidden talents, potential assistance or any number of positive qualities. By joining forces they create an unlikely couple, yet they each know in themselves there is everything to be gained from their union. What might have been barred to one becomes open to the other; if they are united, this opening of doorways brings them both an advantage. The key to their success lies in their mutual encouragement, and their ability to seize opportunities overlooked by others with less perceptive vision.

Conclusion

Venus in Leo indicates loyalty, with close relationships being a matter of self-expression. Leo's corresponding Tarot card, trump XI, Lust, means the reconciliation of opposing forces, the opportunity to advance, use of magical power, great courage. On the Tree of Life the sign and trump occupy the path between the spheres of Mars and Jupiter, called Strength and Mercy respectively. This trump shows how the two should be balanced. The entry of Venus, goddess of love, although indicating a backward step on the Tree, has a quality of such universal importance that it justifies its intrusion. By enhancing the bond between strength and mercy, by underlining their union, the two can proceed to their mutual benefit. When this is translated into daily affairs, it shows upward progress in new and sometimes groundbreaking ways. It is the fire of Venus and the fire of Leo controlled, directed and put to good use.

8 in 6

8=Mercury, 6= the star sign Virgo and Tarot trump IX, The Hermit. Mercury rules the element water, Virgo is of earth.

The Silent Flower

Helpful guidance is a benefit. To act on that guidance is clearly sensible. It matters little if the guidance comes from a small voice within, or a source from outside. If what is heard is undeniably correct, correct action should follow.

A helpful guide is not always heard. A summer flower attracts the bee; neither flower nor bee listens to the other. Yet without mutual cooperation they would perish. The flower can only be a flower; it grows to its fullest glory to win the bee. The bee relies on what it sees and senses in order to thrive. Thus, the miracle begins with the silent flower, the bloom that grows to its fullest glory to win the bee.

It is not helpful to question if flowers came before bees, or bees before flowers. It is only helpful to question why seeing and sensing, or growing to the fullest glory, should be questioned.

Summary

There is guidance available, the signs are obvious and there to see, yet they are not being taken on board. This guidance may take the form of personal development or chance help in revealing a sense of direction. Either way it brings positive advice, helpful clues. Yet there is an element of rejection that prevents acceptance. The oracle's last paragraph raises the issue of questioning past events leading up to the present, and how pieces of the puzzle are being scrutinized for faults. It is as though one is determined to find errors where they do not exist. This is not timid dithering; it is a fear of truth, a reluctance to admit that the signs are correct. When contributing factors are seen to be as obvious and meaningful as they are, it is not helpful to question them.

Conclusion

Mercury in Virgo indicates a tendency to plough deep into matters of trivial importance. This anxiety to penetrate the minutiae of detail is clearly not to be welcomed in most daily affairs, leading as it does to the shelving of more important issues. Virgo's corresponding Tarot card, trump IX, The Hermit, means isolation or withdrawal, discretion, careful planning, also spiritual illumination from within. These factors are not helped by the entrance of a fleeting and cold-blooded planet. On the Tree of Life the sign and trump occupy a path below the sphere of Mercury, which would normally suggest a step up when that planet enters the world of a lower trump. But The Hermit is not sufficiently developed; it is too inert to handle the swift and cutting energies. The oracle is a warning to beware finicky distractions and keep matters in perspective. Do not be side-tracked by excessively analytical considerations when the real solution is obvious. It is the water of Mercury muddying the earth of Virgo.

9 in 7

9=Luna, 7=the star sign Libra and Tarot trump VIII, Adjustment. Luna rules the element air, Libra is of air.

End of Decrease

The universe evolves from chaos to order by inevitable degrees. When order is established, the universe will return to chaos. All things are allotted to their season. It is like the pair of balances, which tilt first one way and then the other, as they weigh the shift of all creation. Always and forever, the sum of the balances remains unchanged. The tilt they display is the heartbeat of creation.

As above, so below. Our affairs wax and wane; the small becomes great, and then greatness diminishes. The cycles of change advance regardless of our desire. When decrease comes it must reach its lowest ebb; nothing can prevent the cycles of change. Reassurance comes from knowing that every decrease has its ending. From the lowest ebb, new growth springs.

Advantage is gained by planning for the effects of decline, for then resources are protected and nothing is lost. To stand and survey the end of decrease, is to stand in a position of strength.

Summary

Libra is the sign of the balances, or scales as they are more commonly known. This oracle is of a cautionary nature, in that it speaks of a cycle of change which cannot be avoided: 'All things are allotted to their season'. The present cycle is one of reduction, the inevitable consequence of matters already in motion and which, through their advanced state, are almost impossible to reverse. The only escape might be the introduction of substantial new resources, the 'planning for the effects of decline', but the advice should rather be taken to mean the tactics necessary to insulate what is already on hand. None of this is a criticism of prior conduct leading to an avoidable calamity. It is a statement of fact, a lesson in life itself, where decay must follow growth. The light on the horizon is that the decrease is ending, and in this sense it is an oracle of optimism. From here the next cycle of growth appears.

Conclusion

Luna in Libra indicates a desire for harmony in personal relationships, plus a sense of security through actions taken in the past. The latter is in tune with the closing advice of the oracle, but the Tree of Life allows a more detailed look at this astrological view of star sign and planet. Libra's corresponding Tarot card, trump VIII, Adjustment, indicates treaties, the formation of partnerships, marriage, negotiations, vindication of truth. All these can be seen to demand a balanced approach, which is the underlying meaning of the card's title. Yet the entrance of Luna, with its powerful ability to bring deception and illusion, does nothing to support this balance. The air of Luna combines with the air of Libra to drum winds of change that tilt the scales. When balance is disturbed there will be gains and losses before stability returns. In this instance, the downward swing is almost over and a return to stability is the next phase. It is the air of Luna and the air of Libra reducing to a breeze after combining in a squall.

3 in 8

3= Saturn, 8= the star sign Scorpio and Tarot trump XIII, Death. Saturn rules the element water, Scorpio is of water.

Stillness

When all things reduce to stillness, when the crop itself cannot grow, there will be no gathering of a useful harvest.

The harvester sits unmoving when the fields are not ripe. His scythe stays at his side, its keen edge waiting. In the darkness of night he dwells upon the mysteries, seeking answers. He sees the moon in her courses, passing from east to west, and the stars that follow her example, drifting across the heavens. He ponders over the motions above and the stillness below. He asks why his affairs remain unmoving. He asks why the heavens thrive.

With the coming of dawn, light and warmth will bring their changes. If the fields have been sown and watered in their season, the harvester may yet take up his scythe.

Summary

This oracle points to a situation in which events over a period of time, if allowed to proceed without due care, will terminate in stagnation. Like a field of corn unable to ripen, no good will come of it. The field's owner, 'the harvester' has nothing to harvest, and his expectations of a useful crop are dashed. There is no sign here of any immediate benefit, only a search for reasons why matters have come to this disappointing pass. Yet this harvester is no fool, for no fool rises to own land with potential. He has a wealth of opportunity before him, none of which will be realised in the absence of attendant care.

This is not the inevitable outcome of unavoidable cycles of change; this is more the cost of being lax in attention and forethought.

Conclusion

Saturn is a slow-moving planet. The changes it brings do not happen overnight, and the warnings should have been apparent for a while. Saturn in Scorpio traditionally indicates the desire to control circumstances for personal gain, which really is no more than most working people must do every day of their lives. On the Tree of Life, Saturn is a lofty sphere commanding respect, whereas Tarot trump XIII, Death, has a poor choice of title: one thing it does not mean is the grim reaper! The card refers to a state of change, transformation, passing from one condition to another – not the cessation of life. One of the powerful effects of Saturn is to bring affairs to a halt. Hence we see that 'all things reduce to stillness', and the figure of Time in the card slows down accordingly. Nothing seems to move and there is no progress, only stagnation. Whether this can be reversed depends entirely on whether the 'fields have been sown and watered in their season'. If steps have been taken to ensure that everything that could be done has been done, then circumstances may yet be restarted. If not, there will be no harvest in this direction. The waters of Saturn and Scorpio will combine in a rank and unmoving lake.

4 in 9

4=Jupiter, 9 =the star sign Sagittarius and Tarot trump XIV, Art. Jupiter rules the element water, Sagittarius is of fire.

United Effort

Art is the balancing of space and colour, the crafting of stone into pleasing form, the creation of substance from a vision. Art is the great transformer. When a pleasing vision is turned into substance, to touch that vision is a tribute to art.

To unlock pleasure from places where potential exists, it is helpful to understand the mixing of materials, how to combine and arrange them. The arrow finding its mark is a skill; seeing the bow and the arrow in the prisons of their boughs, setting them free and giving them life, is an art. The archer and the bow maker rely on each other. Without their united effort the arrow would not find its mark.

Summary

This oracle is a tribute to the process of creative and imaginative thought. Although it speaks in terms of the visual arts, it should be viewed in the sense of arranging private affairs in an inspiring way. Inspiring, that is, not only for the creator but also for those who look on or who are otherwise involved. When the oracle speaks of crafting a pleasing form from stone, or releasing a bow and arrow from their prisons of wood (i.e. the uncut bough), it is promoting the need to see opportunities at a crude and early stage, and turning them to personal advantage. It further advises that more than one pair of hands is usually necessary to create a work of art; artists rarely make their raw materials or tools, for example. In a similar way, for the arrow to find its mark (or the desired objective to be secured) it takes a united effort, and that has its part to play in the direction indicated here.

Conclusion

Jupiter in Sagittarius indicates activity and enthusiasm, sometimes with a touch of impatience. The star sign's corresponding Tarot card, trump XIV, Art, indicates harmonious partnerships, control of volatile situations, success. All these are qualities which could be ruined by the entrance of the wrong planet, but Jupiter acts as a beneficial force, bringing stability to partnerships and calming volatile situations. On the Tree of Life the sign and trump are on the middle pillar, beneath the Sun. This is an auspicious starting-point, and the entrance of Jupiter signals a direct route to a high point of aspiration. The figure in the trump, carefully blending her materials in the cauldron of her craft, hits upon a winning combination. The result is success. It is the fire of Sagittarius, encouraged by the Sun, bringing warmth to the beneficial waves of Jupiter.

5 in 10

5= Mars, 10 = the star sign Capricorn and Tarot trump XV, The Devil. Mars rules the element fire, Capricorn is of earth.

Unrelenting Steps

The mountain goat works hard to survive. The slopes are steep, the elements unkind. To reach the summit in search of nourishment demands constant toil. When the slopes are approached with enthusiasm and vigour the toil is not diminished, but it passes with easier steps. When the high peak is held firmly in view, obstacles and hurdles will not endure. Success follows unrelenting steps.

No one can approach a mountain unaware of its height. The slopes are plain to see. Therefore, the enormity of an assault upon the peak cannot be underestimated. There will be no unexpected toil.

When enthusiasm and vigour fuel the journey, the peak is gained without avoidable delay. There is no weakening of inner resolve, and a work of endurance will be accomplished. The mountain goat will stand aloft, master of the mountain.

Summary

The mountain goat is an image of someone down-to-earth, and not dismayed by the prospect of working for as long as it takes to secure an ambition. They are hardy in the face of adversity, yet quick thinking and quick to seize their chance. There is considerable energy at work here, a powerful drive to achieve the desired goal. That goal is represented by a mountain. No mountain can be underestimated; therefore the size of the task ahead will not have gone unnoticed. But the odds against will not deter someone with the skills and determination to succeed. There is little in the way of good luck about this; it is down to effort, making the right moves at the right time and without any thought of giving up.

Conclusion

Mars in Capricorn indicates a passion for power and control. It is the warrior energy of Mars at its best, when applied in the right direction. Capricorn's corresponding Tarot card, trump XV, The Devil, indicates hidden forces at work, secret activities, unscrupulous methods, the need to raise basic driving forces to serve a higher purpose. Capricorn is the sign of the goat, and the figure on trump XV is similarly horned, underlining their link. The path they occupy on the Tree of Life is relatively low, with Mars slightly above them. The planet symbolizes a stage of development that must be passed on the way to a higher success. The entrance of Mars at the present time therefore suggests a goal or ambition realised; it is the fire of Mars warming the earth of Capricorn to an exalted state.

6 in 11

6= Sun, 11= the star sign Aquarius and Tarot trump XVII, The Star. Sun rules the element air, Aquarius is of air.

New Life

The waterfall flows by day and night. In the night it shines with light from the stars, by day it is warmed by the sun. Ever moving, it is lit from above.

The waterfall feeds the stream, the stream feeds the oceans. Fresh water becomes salt. In the oceans life is abundant; in a stream it is sparse. When the fresh water changes, new life celebrates. Ever moving, lit from above and promoting new life, a waterfall is like inspiration. Without inspiration there is no advance, no improvement. Old ways are not transformed. Darkness triumphs.

When the sun shines on a waterfall, illumination is at its height. There is no finer condition, no better way to promote new life.

Summary

The waterfall is a symbol of life itself, ever moving, always changing. When the 'fresh water becomes salt', or life meets an ultimate objective, the changes we have worked for are accomplished and 'new life celebrates'. The parallels with inspiration are apposite, in that without the inspiration to advance and develop, without the desire to improve our lot we would remain static, gaining nothing and going nowhere. Sometimes the best ideas seem to spring out of nowhere, and we wonder if we have been prompted by something or someone 'up above'. Most people can recall a situation where events seemed to be inspired by helpful but unseen forces. In this oracle of good omen, the sun shining on a waterfall presages the most favourable conditions for progress.

Conclusion

Sun in Aquarius indicates an inventive mind, and the need to participate in wider social circles. The star sign's corresponding Tarot card, trump XVII, The Star, means the expansion of horizons, unexpected help, new outlook. The image of a waterfall is suggested by the card, where a female figure holds aloft a cup from which she pours water over herself. A cup held in her other hand is lowered and emptying its contents; the sea is just visible in the distance. The figure is a personification of the divine female principle; she is the goddess made manifest. The water she pours is ethereal, depicting the infinite variations of existence. From the lower cup she pours universal blood, the nectar of creation. By this transformation she makes all manifestation possible. On the Tree of Life the card is between the spheres of Sun and Neptune. The Sun now entering the realm of the card shows that everything is in balance. It is the perfect starting point for forging ahead. The air of Sun and the air of Aquarius combine in complete agreement.

7 in 12

7=Venus, 12= the star sign Pisces and Tarot trump XVIII, The Moon. Venus rules the element fire, Pisces is of water.

Hidden Deeps

A deep river runs slow; in its depths live creatures of many forms. Their heads are in the mud, scavenging. They do not welcome the light of the sun. They are at odds with all humanity, all compassion and virtue. Theirs is a world of darkness and savagery.

Those who walk upon the river bank admire the sun. They bathe in its light and welcome the warmth. They watch the slow river and understand that unseen forms lurk below. Even the vermin fly and mosquito are taken, snapped by jaws as they touch the water. A deep river is merciless. It holds no distinction between one life or another.

No river begins deep. Their origins are in shallow places, where the river bed is visible and nothing can hide. To understand the hidden deeps, it is helpful to return to the source. Only those who care, who feel compassion, will return to the source. Long before they arrive they will have gained many answers. Those who walk on regardless, who stroll the bank with carefree steps, are as one with the river.

Summary

This oracle concerns events slow in the making, slow to build up to a point where it may appear that matters have come to a halt, or that good fortune is lacking. The deep river is a symbol of those events, an image of a world where much seems hidden, and in the deeps there are unpleasant surprises waiting to happen. The concept of creatures with their 'heads in the mud, scavenging' is a strong image of those out to cause harm in some way with scant regard for how they achieve their objective. But this is likely to be an unfounded fear. The deep river is a mass of deception and self-doubt. To back-track, or to 'return to the source', is a certain way to understand the nature of these doubts. By understanding them they will cease to wield their power.

Conclusion

Understanding is a merit of Venus in Pisces, along with sympathy and compassion. The star sign's corresponding Tarot card, trump XVIII, The Moon, is a rather ominous portrayal of falsehood, deception and "the darkest hour before the dawn". The entry of Venus into the realm of this trump is a particularly good omen. On the Tree of Life Venus is the planet to which the trump aspires, and its entry now therefore signals the achievement of an objective. Circumstances may be dark and uncertain, but with adequate thought and consideration – and the determination not to be unsettled by doubt or misunderstanding – the outcome will be positive. It is a warning not to be bogged down or held back by uncertainty, but to recognise the truth of a situation and brave it out accordingly. It is the fire of Venus warming and encouraging the water of Pisces.

8 in 1

8= Mercury, 1= the star sign Aries and Tarot trump IV, The Emperor. Mercury rules the element water, Aries is of fire.

Haste

The young emperor has secured his throne not by birthright alone, but through the strength of his character and his passion for command. He has no heart for the slow deliberations of counsel; his impulse is to act swiftly and with force. When he displays these qualities in matters of state, the future of the empire is simple to foretell.

The royal advisors gather: what counsel should they offer to one who rises to greatness, only to cloud his reign with unthinking haste?

If the emperor shows restraint he will realise his error. Evidence of his folly will be plain to see. Surrounded by folly, he will not reject good counsel.

In the quiet of his chamber, the emperor must reflect upon the recklessness of unthinking haste. He must learn the value of wise deliberation in every matter of state. By turning his back to his advisors, the empire will fall.

Summary

This is a reference to someone – or perhaps a company or some other collective – that has made good headway through their own efforts. They have not relied on external help so much as their own innate sense of what can be achieved. But now that the throne has been won, or an initial objective secured, a new approach is not only desirable but vital. What served in the past will not serve in the present. It is time to change both the method of action and the way that action is steered. The stated youthfulness of the emperor has little to do with age; it refers more to the new turn of a current situation. For that situation to advance without disappointment, the emperor should adopt advice from trusted sources. If that advice is not taken up, the consequence will be failure.

Conclusion

Mercury in Aries indicates the tendency to form hasty decisions, and to make knee-jerk judgements. The star sign's corresponding Tarot card, trump IV, The Emperor, means energy, rashness, conquest and overweening confidence. On the Tree of Life, Aries and trump IV occupy a relatively low path on which Venus is their next objective. Once the sphere of Venus has been mastered, a crossing to Mercury follows. In this oracle, Venus has been bypassed. Without the acquired warmth of Venus to offset the entrance of swift and emotionless Mercury, that trickster-god holds sway with little to keep him in check. This is not good news for making clear-headed and rational choices. The ego runs rampant, with scant regard for caution or plain commonsense. Remember that this is an indication of what will happen; it is not necessarily a criticism of affairs as they currently stand. It is an advance warning, although there are likely to be trends that display this tendency. Here, the waters of Mercury serve only to anger the fires of Aries.

9 in 2

9= Luna, 2= the star sign Taurus and Tarot trump V, The Hierophant. Luna rules the element air, Taurus is of earth.

Bolder Steps

When enlightenment enters daily affairs, it is like the sun breaking through clouds. The world becomes radiant, the obscure becomes clear.

Shadows from clouds dull the vision. Clouds have no substance, yet they interfere with light and contentment. Clouds manifest in many shapes, appearing as people, seeming like faces. They display colours of great beauty to make the soul marvel, yet still they have no substance. They dissipate, leaving nothing. It is the nature of all deception.

When enlightenment enters daily affairs, we see through the clouds and there are no shadows. It is a welcome marriage, this coming together of inner enlightenment and outward vision. There is no deception, only knowledge.

With knowledge we walk with bolder steps. The roses with thorns and the roses without thorns are seen where they prosper.

Summary

The underlying spirit of this oracle is in the line, 'it is like the sun breaking through clouds'. Where circumstances were doubtful or unclear, a new light dawns to throw everything in sharp relief. This is conveyed by use of the word enlightenment, which will probably have more to do with clarifying a situation rather than any spiritual connotations. The clouds are passing fantasies, dreams without foundation. Although beguiling enough to 'make the soul marvel' they interfere with reality and then simply fade away. Their passing is no bad thing. Free from their influence, there is no more deception. Their place is taken by a vision that perceives with more accuracy. The roses with thorns are potential dangers, while the roses without thorns are attractive options with no hidden drawbacks. They can be seen for what they are, and where they are. There will be no more falling prey to deception, from whatever source it might come.

Conclusion

Luna in Taurus indicates a profound understanding of the values of life, plus a strong sense of security. The star sign's corresponding Tarot card, trump V, The Hierophant, means stubborn strength, endurance, goodness of heart, patience and peace. It is a card that links to secrets made manifest. On the Tree of Life, Luna occupies an important place on the middle pillar. It is the dark sphere of the mind, where both inspiration and nightmare have their roots. Luna is often associated with madness – hence the word lunatic – but given the right circumstances it is a potent force for good. Superficially, the entrance of Luna would suggest a markedly backward step (it is far below the trump) but when Luna enters the world of The Hierophant, it is very like the joining of parted souls. There are various esoteric reasons for this, which have no real place in this Conclusion, but they are suggested by the rose (a feminine symbol) behind the hierophant's head, and the nine nails above that rose – nine being the number of feminine Luna. The entry of Luna is thus a 'welcome marriage', bringing fresh insights to life and making clear the way ahead. It is the uplifting air of Luna making more fertile and productive the gentle earth of Taurus.

3 in 3

3= Saturn, 3= the star sign Gemini and Tarot trump VI, The Lovers. Saturn rules the element water, Gemini is of air.

Firm Foundations

When two become one, harmony, balance and agreement triumph. Their union is not marked by a storm of sudden change, nor is there the collapse of long-established order. Sudden change and collapse are the products of conflict; they have no place in a bonding by accord.

The joining of two in an agreeable manner presages the foundation of order. When order arises from an accord, it continues without harmful dispute. Hastily built is hastily fallen; stability is the child of serenity.

In times of stability it is appropriate to arrange affairs with care and attention, and to shelter all resources. This ensures the continual spread of firm foundations, from which further heights can be reached in safety.

Summary

This oracle may refer to two people, or to one person and their desired objective. In either case, circumstances are such that it is the right time for the union to take place. The oracle points out that there will be no sudden change or collapse of an existing situation, for the overall nature of this union does not evoke that kind of backlash or reaction. The image overall is of measured progress, where matters come together without dissent or obstruction. Calmly and evenly, events proceed according to plan.

Conclusion

Saturn in Gemini indicates a marked increase in mental activity, aimed at the achievement of ambitions. This is due largely to Gemini being an airy sign, and air by tradition is a symbol for the process of thought, while Saturn displays powerful decisive qualities. On the Tree of Life, Saturn occupies a highly important position. The planet's mystical powers are immense, and when these enter Tarot trump VI, The Lovers, it is possible to extract a deep significance. The card is an image of action and reaction, analysis and synthesis. In this sense it is allied to alchemy, the raising of low matter into gold. On the paths of the Tree, this search for perfection is achieved by The Lovers in the sphere of Saturn – the card actually aspires to this sphere. The fact that Saturn has now entered the situation indicates an objective won, which explains the oracle's optimistic view. Action and reaction have ceased to be; there is only union and harmony. The low matter has been transformed into gold. This is the basis for a prediction of 'firm foundations', and 'bonding by accord'. The advice to shelter resources is not a warning of lurking disaster, but a caution against overconfidence allowing hard-earned benefits to slip away. It is the water of Saturn uplifting the air of Gemini.

4 in 4

4= Jupiter, 4= the star sign Cancer and Tarot trump VII, The Chariot. Jupiter rules the element water, Cancer is of water.

Pleasure

The charioteer does not remain in familiar lands. It is his destiny to move on. He crosses borders and boundaries; bravely he enters the unknown. His strength is the strength of conviction, his journey a mark of his will to succeed.

There are times when the charioteer must pause; he must rest and take stock. There will be days when he finds no place of welcome, and he must retrace his steps to start afresh. Opportunities move like the wind, and he must be as the wind, altering direction. Failure would be to remain where he is, to stay where there is no benefit, or to advance where there is no benefit.

By altering direction and retracing his steps, the charioteer will meet with lands and people he knows well. It will be of advantage to share his experience, to listen to their knowledge of places he does not recognise. When he hears of a realm fit for him, he will sense the beginnings of pleasure. When he starts out anew his pleasure will magnify.

Summary

The charioteer in this instance is either a person or a method of working. It is the symbol of a driving force; something or someone not prone to taking it easy. It is activity and energy, rolling ever onwards. Sometimes in life this approach can be overwhelming, and on those occasions it is necessary to step back and review the situation. Forging ahead regardless does not bring any advantage. The message here is that the direction indicated is not fortuitous, yet all is not lost. The charioteer is resourceful, and knowing that one road ahead is a dead end will only inspire the search for another and better road. It is far from being over; it is simply that this is not the ideal way forward.

Conclusion

Jupiter in Cancer indicates the tendency to share acquired knowledge, usually through close relationships. The star sign's corresponding Tarot card, trump VII, The Chariot, indicates triumph, hope, obedience and faithfulness. These are all admirable qualities, yet Jupiter represents a stage on the Tree of Life through which the charioteer, on his ascent to the spiritual heights, has already passed. It represents a minor backward step, and the oracle's advice is that it should be undertaken in the form of a review, a refresher course in lessons, skills or experiences previously acquired. It is fortunate, in some ways, that Jupiter is the planet to enter the trump's world. The beneficial aspects of Jupiter ensure that no harm befalls the charioteer. The planet's stabilizing energies will act as a benevolent support, a powerful and welcome aid. Once the reassessment of available options is complete, the journey can begin once more with an improved chance of success. The water of Jupiter and the waters of Cancer combine in a wave of gathering strength.

5 in 5

5= Mars, 5=the star sign Leo and Tarot trump XI, Lust.
Mars rules the element fire, Leo is of fire.

Turmoil

Courage and strength, energy and action; these are the builders of cities. When there is turmoil and the labourers in the streets are not at peace, courage, strength, energy and action will restore control and see the city built.

Turmoil must have a reason. In the face of so many, courage is needed to face that reason. The answer will be found in weakness, for turmoil is a product of weakness. Without order there is no power of restraint or guidance. Without guidance there is no unified purpose, and the weak take advantage of freedom from purpose. The building of the city becomes threatened by their weakness.

Courage, strength, energy and action; at the hub of turmoil these will stand victorious.

Summary

This oracle is a lesson in fortitude. Firmness of mind is an integral part of any endeavour. The city is a symbol for that endeavour, in whatever form it might take. Turmoil, or more likely a sense of confusion surrounding an issue, will naturally oppose any progress. The restraint suggested as necessary should be understood as the application of guidelines, the defining of basic principles and direction. There is no criticism here of the endeavour itself, if anything the oracle's advice gives supportive backing. The overall tone is of a situation where there are initial difficulties, including some friction, which are seemingly inevitable. By taking control, the ground is cleared for onward progress.

Conclusion

Mars in Leo indicates strong passions and a firm determination to succeed. Leo's corresponding Tarot card, trump XI, Lust, means the reconciliation of opposing forces, the opportunity to advance, great courage. All these are elements found in the oracle. The initial confusion and friction stems from the entrance of Mars into the world of the trump. On the Tree of Life, Mars is the starting point from which the Tarot characters set out to approach the sphere of Jupiter. The appearance of Mars at the present time therefore indicates that everything is as it should be. Yet Mars has disruptive powers. The warlike forces represented by that planet must be mastered before the journey to benevolent Jupiter can begin. The dominance of Mars indicates those forces rule and they will create initial difficulties. But the Tarot card is the most powerful of those associated with the zodiac, and it will not be overwhelmed so easily. Mars will be put in its place. The friction or confusion will be overcome and from that point a calmer journey gets underway. It is the fire of Mars aggravating the fire of Leo.

6 in 6

6= Sun, 6= the star sign Virgo and Tarot trump IX, The Hermit. Sun rules the element air, Virgo is of earth.

The Open Door

The hermit has built his place of learning. The hermitage is well prepared; there is light within and light from outside. The door is open.

Doors are closed for protection or privacy; when there is no threat of danger, or secrecy has no part to play, keeping the door open welcomes the world.

The hermit's lamp remains on the table, its light is not allowed to die. The hermit knows darkness will follow light, and the kindled lamp is his eternal safeguard. Those who are always prepared do not stumble on unseen obstacles.

The hermit attends to his learning. Peace fills his place of study.

Summary

The tone of this oracle is that of optimism. The hermit is a symbol for a person or situation in which various matters are obscure yet indicate no risk. The hermit has 'built his place of learning' – the hermitage – and we are told that it is well prepared. This means that he enjoys a secure and appropriate position, and the open door is a way of affirming that security. There is a clear view ahead, and the surrounding landscape shows no sign of hazard. There is every reason to feel confident. The lamp that remains on the table is the hermit's precious guiding light; it is his source of inner awareness and his personal yardstick for deciding on important issues. By upholding his deepest convictions he will not make errors, or 'stumble on unseen obstacles'. He can go about his intended business with confidence.

Conclusion

Sun in Virgo indicates a tendency to control or organize personal surroundings and issues. The star sign's corresponding Tarot card, trump IX, The Hermit, means a need for isolation or withdrawal, discretion, careful planning, illumination from within. On the Tree of Life the card occupies the path from Sun to the sphere of Jupiter. This tells us that in this oracle, the figure in the card is exactly where it should be. The energies of Sun bring balance and harmony through a process of synthesis, or combining various ideas into a working whole. That synthesis is now in full swing. The path occupied by The Hermit leads to benevolent Jupiter, with its overtones of mercy and stability. There is little to suggest any imbalance leading to difficulties ahead, and provided the vital 'lamp' is never extinguished, the open door heralds a satisfying achievement. It is the air of Sun elevating the earth of Virgo.

7 in 7

7=Venus, 7= the star sign Libra and Tarot trump VIII, Adjustment. Venus rules the element fire, Libra is of air.

Cutting Through

This perceptive lady carries scales to make her judgements. The sword she bears wins respect. Her sword has never known anger; it serves to cut through confusion. When the lady decides, few choose to argue.

The lady proceeds by weighing facts, balancing truth against deceit. Yet judging the scales is not easy. One fact can outweigh another; who can tell which of the two facts is preferable? The facts must be judged for themselves. When the judgement is complete their hidden merit, not the open facts, can be weighed in the scales. In the same way truth may outweigh deception; yet a small deception can mask a larger truth. All deceptions have their role to fill, they are not without purpose. That is why the lady bears her sword. That is why she must cut through confusion, before her scales can truly balance.

Summary

The lady of this oracle represents a position where care is definitely required. There is no suggestion of danger, only the need for a thorough appraisal of the situation. The circumstances do not have to be complex, but such as they are they represent the possibility of ambitions without foundation, hopes without the means of seeing them through, or an opportunity that is not quite as it seems. The oracle labours the point of judging the true value of available or perceptible facts, and taking a closer look at what, in some way, appears to be a façade. It is no coincidence that the lady has both a sword and scales. The scales are an automatic or superficial means of summing up; without the sword to cut through confusion beforehand, there would be very little of true value to weigh. Realising what is beneficial, even if it conflicts with first impressions, must come before making a commitment.

Conclusion

Venus in Libra indicates the desire to perfect personal relationships. The star sign's corresponding Tarot card, trump VIII, Adjustment, means treaties, the formation of partnerships, marriage, negotiations, the vindication of truth. On the Tree of Life the card is above the sphere of Venus, and the renewed entry of that planet suggests a slightly retrograde step. The inherent qualities of Venus serve to dampen any likelihood of damage; it translates as a need to pause and reflect on basic principles, rather than forge ahead with every confidence. The sword carried by the lady is a symbol for the dissecting or analytical facility of practical thought. It is thought, tempered by heart-felt considerations, that needs to be applied in this case. When it has, few will 'choose to argue'. It is the fire of Venus helpfully warning the air of Libra.

8 in 8

8=Mercury, 8=the star sign Scorpio and Tarot trump XIII, Death. Mercury rules the element air, Scorpio is of water.

Assessment

The harvester is surveying his field. He assesses the ripeness of the crop, and he sees it is ready to harvest. He looks to the skies, and evaluates the weather. He judges that conditions are in his favour. He looks to the size of the field, and gauges there is time enough to complete his task before the day's end. Taking up his scythe, he studies the handle and finds it to be stout and firm. The blade is sharp and suited to the labour ahead.

The harvester stands unmoving. He determines the best place to begin, and where he should end. Past experience has taught him to be exact. Knowing where the pitfalls lie, he takes care to avoid them.

There is nothing before him that he does not understand. Gripping his scythe, the harvester moves forward with measured steps.

Summary

The unmistakable tone of this oracle is of care applied to a promising situation. The harvester is leaving nothing to chance. Every aspect of the task ahead is studied, carefully considered and evaluated. These are preliminary steps based on his past experiences. Scrutinizing every move in advance will allow him to harvest his crop with efficiency. A harvester who starts in this way will continue along the same lines; there is no place here for emotional considerations, only the almost surgical precision of calculated action. A harvest approached in this manner is gathered with swift efficiency.

Conclusion

Mercury in Scorpio indicates a strong sense of insight and a passion for exploring mysteries. Scorpio's corresponding Tarot card, trump XIII, Death, means starting afresh, sudden change, transformation. (This card does not refer to physical death, but to the end of one situation and the start of another.) On the Tree of Life the card is slightly above the sphere of Mercury. The reappearance of this planet in the trump suggests a slightly backward step, yet in many ways it is helpful and not in the least detrimental. The oracle makes reference to this when it mentions 'knowing where the pitfalls lie'. The trump is linked to the Hebrew letter Nun, which means fish, the lightning-quick dwellers of deep places, and fish are sacred to Mercury. This close connection between trump and planet allows Mercury, which is swiftness and accuracy of thought, to act unimpeded. There will be action without emotion, but through a meticulous approach the end result will agree with planned intentions.

9 in 9

9=Luna, 9=the star sign Sagittarius and Tarot trump XIV, Art. Luna rules the element air and Sagittarius is of fire.

The Rainbow

After the rain comes the rainbow. It spans the sky, a bridge between worlds. It is a thing of beauty where once there was grey. We do not ask for the rainbow, it is given freely.

Beauty instead of grey; always there is hope for those who raise their eyes. Not asked for but given; always there are gifts for those who are in favour. To know where to raise one's eyes, to know how and of whom to win favour, these are the bricks of the bridge between worlds.

Summary

This rather cryptic oracle is a pointer to the state of mind and attitude required to deal with this situation. It should be read on two levels; spiritual and material. After an unpleasant period (the rain before the rainbow), circumstances change by the unexpected appearance of encouragement. This is earned by those who do not give way to feelings of despair, but who maintain their belief that there is help on hand at all times, whether seen or unseen. By being as agreeable as possible to those able to lend a hand, a bridge is built between a need and its solution. It is for the individual to decide how much effort should be spiritual, and how much should be material. What is clear is that a bridge of sorts will need to be found, therefore the future in this case is not without its hurdles. Equally clear is that the oracle is suggesting a way to build that bridge. This means that a positive outcome is within reach.

Conclusion

Luna in Sagittarius indicates a desire to be free from demands and responsibilities. The star sign's corresponding Tarot card, trump XIV, Art, means the joining of forces, harmonious partnerships, control of volatile situations, success. On the Tree of Life the sign and trump occupy the path between Luna and Sun. In this oracle Luna is therefore where it should be, acting as a starting point for the trump, and on the face of it everything should be in order. The problem is that Luna represents a difficult stage on the ascent of the Tree; it is a realm of darkness and illusion, with only flashes of clear light. There is no one better equipped to gain victory over this stage than the figure represented by the card. Welcome sunlight is directly ahead for her. As Luna is the first stage of the Tree to lie beyond the physical world, it is where faith and determination must both play a major part. The rainbow is an image from alchemy, in which base material is transformed into gold, and it has key links with the parallel symbolism of the card. It is a bridge of light, or a gifted opportunity, that will be crossed with the right approach. The air of Luna fans and inspires the fire of Sagittarius.

3 in 10

3=Saturn, 10=the star sign Capricorn and Tarot trump XV, The Devil. Saturn rules the element water, Capricorn is of earth.

Fortunate Days

The mountain goat has climbed so high, the view he enjoys is unequalled. To left and right he finds nourishment. Labour is behind him; ahead there is rest. These are fortunate days for the dweller of rocky slopes.

Who would envy this mountain goat?

He is a horned beast, unkempt and wild. He must work for his comforts, as small as they are. The mountain lion is his enemy, and the scorpion, the cold winds. We do not envy the beast, only his fortunate days. But we cannot part the two.

Good fortune knows no boundaries. All sincere effort is ultimately rewarded. Those who climb to the greatest heights can learn much of value in their unequalled view.

Summary

This oracle speaks of a goal accomplished, and in the process something else is gained. There is a new understanding of matters previously taken for granted, or perhaps even regarded with some disdain. It is as though success has a way of mellowing an outlook, so that thought is given to situations or individuals once deemed undeserving, or who were snubbed so far as due recognition was concerned. The success indicated is no stroke of good luck, but payment for efforts made in the right direction. That payment is considerable and of long-term duration. The 'dweller of the rocky slopes' is an acknowledgement that the road to success was less than even, while the whole image of the mountain goat conveys a sense of practical hard work.

Conclusion

Saturn in Capricorn indicates endurance, and working towards stable achievements. The star sign's associated Tarot card, trump XV, The Devil, means ambition, secret plans, and unscrupulous methods. The entrance of Saturn is a favourable omen. On the Tree of Life Saturn is a lofty sphere, representing a profound level of understanding. In comparison the path of the Tarot trump is quite low, signifying that the influence on the character portrayed by the card is wholly beneficial. It foretells success, and the corresponding development of Saturn's gift of understanding. This will reshape attitudes and lead to a more balanced and fairer approach. Saturn is not always so kindly or rewarding. It has such close links with the Tarot character that it is almost a case of destiny reaching an inevitable conclusion.

4 in 11

4= Jupiter, 11= the star sign Aquarius and Tarot trump XVII, The Star. Jupiter rules the element water, Aquarius is of air.

Abundance

Rainfall is the water of life. Without rainfall the fields would parch and turn to dust, the rivers would dry and lakes would empty. Life on land would perish. When the rainfall is glorious, life is glorious.

The sky showers the earth with kindness and brings abundance. People thrive and life becomes full. Like the lakes and rivers, people are free to draw on their store of goodness; they relish the fruits of abundance.

The world is safer when the rainfall is glorious. New growth forges prosperity, prosperity brings joy. There are those who can look to the rainfall and see beyond the rain. They know the true meaning of a heavenly gift; they understand the subtle ways of creation. They are people who walk with nature as a friend.

Summary

Although this oracle speaks of rain, it is actually describing the appearance of benefits that seem to come like a shower. Hence, 'When the rainfall is glorious, life is glorious.' The fruits of abundance and the new growth are images of benefits translating into material gains. The underlying thrust is that of increase and happiness. Those who can 'look to the rainfall and see beyond the rain' are people with the ability to pick up on signals, and see for themselves which way events are heading. They can see too the implication of an event; who or what is probably behind it, and why. Life is an endless array of signposts, but few take the trouble to read them. Appreciating the mystery of things adds to the 'rainfall', bringing contentment through a fuller appreciation of life's driving forces.

Conclusion

Jupiter in Aquarius indicates a desire to be more open minded and seek out new contacts. The star sign's corresponding Tarot card, trump XVII, The Star, means the expansion of horizons, increased vigour, new outlook. On the Tree of Life the sign and trump are above the sphere of Jupiter, the entry of which should indicate a backward step; but Jupiter shares an identity with Poseidon, the Olympian god of the sea, and so has an affinity with The Star, which in turn is linked to the creation concept of the Great Sea. The Star brings manifestation, produces form, and is an image of the Mother Goddess. With the entrance of potent Jupiter, she creates all the positive trends indicated by the oracle. In short, aspirations become reality.

5 in 12

5= Mars, 12=the star sign Pisces and Tarot trump XVIII, The Moon. Mars rules the element fire, Pisces is of water.

The Alley

Tall buildings rise either side of the long and narrow alley. It is night and the alley is unlit. The air is polluted with fear.

In the doorways of the buildings figures stand waiting. They have eyes like animals.

Who will walk alone down this alley? If the journey must be taken, what qualities should the traveller possess?

No one enters such places without vital necessity. Only those in need will choose to walk alone down this alley.

A will strong as iron, a determination to uphold inner strength, a firm resolve to continue to the end; these are qualities the traveller with vital necessity should possess.

Yet this traveller must leave if many figures step from their doorways.

Summary

The alley is a treacherous path ahead. The figures standing in the doorways are dangers, poised and waiting. They are not at some great distance, but close by and therefore all the more worrying. The oracle makes no mention of an imminent assault or attack, only the threat that this could happen if those lying in wait somehow see their obvious and dangerous potential challenged. Those who walk down that alley do so at their risk, for no one is forcing them. Whether or not the figures step out seems for them a matter of choice. This suggests that their reaction depends on how they perceive the traveller. It is the traveller's attitude or approach that matters. The advice to leave if many figures step out means that the traveller is in no position to overwhelm them.

Conclusion

Mars in Pisces indicates a tendency to proceed without a controlled direction. The star sign's associated Tarot card, trump XVIII, The Moon, means illusion, deceit, a crisis of faith, the brink. On the Tree of Life the trump is several steps below the sphere of Mars. The entrance of a higher planet would normally translate in favourable terms as a step up, but Mars is not, for this trump, a favourable planet. The trump is a gloomy and ominous portrayal of the "darkest hour before the dawn", during which time many fears and hurdles must be faced. The military Mars is good for making bold the person facing that task, but it also emboldens the surrounding and greater dangers. Everything simply goes up a notch, and into the mix is added the disruptive fury of the red planet, to be shared by all. The figures in doorways are a reflection of Pisces, which means fishes. They are dwellers of the deep, not given to exposed or open places, which is why the oracle sees them as hidden away. Slippery and cold, these figures are anything but helpful. The fire of Mars serves to muddy the waters of Aquarius.

6 in 1

6=Sun, 1= the star sign Aries and Tarot trump IV, The Emperor. Sun rules the element air, Aries is of fire.

Improvements

An empire is a reflection of its emperor. When the emperor is gifted and prudent, expansion and progress are achieved throughout his realm.

This emperor stands at the threshold of new and important developments. Through his watchful labour he reaches a peak of his reign. Diligence and firmness bring their reward. Improvements come.

From ambition he passes into certainty. He gains advantage from opportunities great and small. Tribute is paid to those who succeed in this way; he will be admired as a worthy leader of his people.

Success must not lead this emperor to abandon all caution. He should continue with conduct appropriate to his status. With diligence this emperor will build a lasting empire on the foundations of the old.

Summary

The Tarot emperor is often a temperamental character, not given to acting with care or thought for others. The oracle speaks of his empire as being a reflection of himself, in other words, the circumstances surrounding him reflect his conduct and the way people react to him. In the present case the emperor is conducting himself in a positive way, and in a manner likely to bring a positive reward. An objective shows every sign of being won. The sphere of that objective is one representing harmony and balance, a definite improvement, and this explains why the oracle says, 'he will be admired as a worthy leader of his people.' Harmony and balance suggest the emperor has mellowed, to the approval and possible relief of those close at hand. One caution is that the emperor should not slip back to his old ways; continuing in his new vein will 'build a lasting empire on the foundations of the old'. All this must be qualified by allowing that the emperor may not refer to a person, but to the circumstances surrounding a particular situation, in which case all the same positive trends will still apply.

Conclusion

Sun in Aries indicates the desire to widen social circles and increase communications. The star sign's corresponding Tarot card, trump IV, The Emperor, means aspiration, vigour, rule and conquest, a person tending to a quarrelsome attitude. On the Tree of Life the sign and trump occupy a relatively low position, between Earth and Venus. The entrance of Sun is a signal that a significant advance has been achieved, in that the higher aspected Sun energies now fill the emperor's environment. These are energies of synthesis, the grouping of things into a larger and coherent whole, which is why he will 'gain advantage from opportunities great and small'. It is impossible to imagine these constructive and welcome energies existing in a situation devoid of success. The air of Sun breathes progress into the leaping fire of Aries.

7 in 2

7=Venus, 2= the star sign Taurus and Tarot trump V, The Hierophant. Venus rules the element fire, Taurus is of earth.

Devotion

There are bonds that restrain and bonds that unite. The bonds that restrain are hammered on anvils, shaped by a craving to control. The bonds that unite are spun from dreams, holding yet not restricting, holding without visible shape. They cannot rust and may last an eternity.

Without shape, lasting for eternity, the invisible is stronger than the visible. When the devoted submit to invisible bonds, their hearts are peaceful. They know the certainty of the bonds, and they know the truth of that to which they are bound. It is their dream made manifest.

No one can know the substance of these bonds. No anvil can shape them. The world turns on, enhanced by the invisible.

Summary

When a dream is made real, either in the form of a person or objective, and that person or objective responds by formulating the same dream, the connection possesses extraordinary strength. Between two people this would undoubtedly surface as love. In the world of commerce or industry it would manifest as the joining of forces, generating a new and enthusiastic thrust towards a shared goal. The dream in either case is not an idle reverie but a clearly defined subject. The way to make that dream come true is not through formal contracts ('bonds that restrain') or dry legal arrangements and the like, but by a passionate will to become one with that dream, as is the case here. The world turns on; the dream becomes real.

Conclusion

Venus in Taurus indicates a desire for permanent relationships, also the acquisition of material goods. The star sign's corresponding Tarot card, trump V, The Hierophant, means stubborn strength, toil, wise counsel, peace. There is a strong affinity between this trump and Venus, for the planet rules the sign of Taurus. The positive aspects of Venus are therefore seen to dominate, and the wise Tarot character is seen to respond by allowing his heart to rule his head. He is not overwhelmed by this, for he is too strong a character, but he is prepared to drop his usual guard and let matters take their course for a time. He is wise enough to know that in this case it is appropriate. It is the fire of Venus stirring the willing earth of Taurus.

8 in 3

8= Mercury, 3= the star sign Gemini and Tarot trump VI, The Lovers. Mercury rules the element air, Gemini is of air.

Necessary Duty

It is the way of lovers to share their hearts. When they suppress their hearts and share their minds, they do so only in the face of adversity. Then they act as one, not with warmth and feeling, but in the swift execution of a necessary duty.

Adversity is ever changing, adopting many forms. Yet always it opposes tranquility. The sharing of hearts cannot dismiss adversity; hearts look inward, the adversity is outside. If the adversity was from within, there would be no sharing of minds. The lovers' minds would be divided. Therefore, the adversity is outside.

A heart suppressed still beats and warms. The lovers will find their union strengthened when tranquility returns.

Summary

The lovers may refer to two people, or to one person and their desired aim. The oracle speaks of a cold phase where feelings must be laid aside and a problem faced, or a difficulty resolved, by astute planning. It is an oracle of optimism; there is no warning of failure or rejection, as confirmed by the last line. The positive aspect throughout is that the lovers act as one. The goal they have in sight is the same goal. They work together, each contributing their best efforts, to reach a conclusion which is to their mutual benefit.

Conclusion

Mercury in Gemini indicates flexibility of ideas and the stimulation of thought. The star sign's corresponding Tarot card, trump VI, The Lovers, means intuition, intelligence and adaptability. Although the trump is above the sphere of Mercury on the Tree of Life, and should indicate a retrograde step when that planet intrudes, there is a sympathetic connection between the planet and trump for Mercury rules the sign of Gemini. The net effect is not to derail or hold back developments but to modify the way they proceed. Mercury is very much the communicator and messenger, and the qualities of applied thought will be uppermost. This suggests a phase where a level-headed approach is necessary rather than any emotional involvement. Mercury is a swift moving planet; the likelihood is that this phase will be of short duration. It is the air of Mercury and the air of Gemini combining into a cutting edge.

9 in 4

9=Luna, 4= the star sign Cancer and Tarot trump VII, The Chariot. Luna rules the element air, Cancer is of water.

Stealth

The charioteer steps down from his chariot. Taking the reins, he leads his horses on foot. The light is good, but the way is difficult. There are rocks and crevices.

His journey is of importance and he must go forward. He will cross this terrain with steadiness and care, leading by hand that which once carried him along.

Like a hunter, he moves with stealth. His horses must not stumble and fall. With his gaze ever ahead he plots his course. This journey of importance demands patience.

The charioteer is armoured and strong. He does not recognise fear. His steeds place their trust in him, and the chariot will not be broken.

Summary

The overall tone of this oracle is one of caution, not retreat. There are many difficulties ahead, although as they are visible ('the light is good') it is not a case of unexpected hurdles. It is a bad stage where action must be appropriate to the moment. The horses and chariot represent close associates or personal resources on which the charioteer once relied for support. Now, however, he must take care of them, and steer them through this difficult time. 'His steeds place their trust in him, and the chariot will not be broken' is a comment on the charioteer's ability to lead the way without encountering disaster; he is a figure worthy of trust and respect. It is a testing time, yet there is nothing here to overwhelm him. His armour, steeds and chariot are the mark of a champion, not of a person without substance.

Conclusion

Luna in Cancer indicates the desire to create a home, and to support close contacts. The star sign's corresponding Tarot card, trump VII, The Chariot, means success through initiative, faithfulness and hope. On the Tree of Life the star sign and trump are considerably above the sphere of Luna. This is a sign that matters are out of place, yet not as bad as they might be. Cancer is the house of Luna, so there is something of a supporting role played by the planet. Although it is in the wrong place at this time its damaging effects are drastically reduced, almost as if feeling rather awkward about the intrusion. The charioteer cannot proceed at his usual fast pace, but he can still go forward. There is likely to be a good background reason for this state of affairs; the character portrayed by the trump is not prone to errors of judgement that lead him into difficulty. It is the air of Luna disturbing the water of Cancer.

3 in 5

3= Saturn, 5= the star sign Leo and Tarot trump XI, Lust.
Saturn rules the element water, Leo is of fire.

Beyond Reach

The naked woman is astride the mighty lion; she carefully brings the beast to a halt.

The apparently weak and the manifestly strong were united in a common purpose. Their unlikely combination served them well. Beneath the surface they were equals. Neither was truly stronger or weaker than the other. This gave them advantages over those who saw the appearance, but could not see the real substance.

Yet, their journey in this direction is too ambitious. Their initial drive and vigour will falter; the distance is too great, the quest is beyond reach.

The apparently weak and the manifestly strong must withdraw. The bond between them will remain intact; it is the distance, not the bond, which makes them weary.

The sands of time flow unceasing. There will be other quests, better journeys.

Summary

The apparently weak and the manifestly strong are references to the two characters portrayed by the trump. A naked woman sits astride a fearsome lion, revealing how strength and weakness can be misunderstood when seen at a superficial level. The trump's theme is one of progress through union, but for that progress to reach a successful conclusion the right conditions have to exist. In this instance it is a step too far. There is nothing wrong between the woman and lion, which might indicate two people or one person and their ultimate aim; what is wrong is the choice of action at this time. The advice is not to give up, for that would deny the innate strength of the trump, but to seek another route.

Conclusion

Saturn in Leo indicates a tendency to act in a dictatorial way without consideration for others. The star sign's corresponding Tarot card, trump XI, Lust, means the reconciliation of opposing forces, great courage, the opportunity to advance. The entrance of Saturn into the world of this trump disturbs the balance between the two figures. Although occupying a high position on the Tree of Life, Saturn has crossed a line for this particular pair. The woman and lion have need of an essential freedom from restraint; there is an air of divine intoxication and ecstasy about them. Ponderous Saturn dampens this by imposing limits and restriction, hence the oracle's warning. It is the water of Saturn dousing the fire of Leo.

4 in 6

4= Jupiter, 6= the star sign Virgo and Tarot trump IX, The Hermit. Jupiter rules the element water, Virgo is of earth.

True Authority

The hermit has drunk deep from the well of knowledge. Useful lessons have been learned. It is time for him to leave the hermitage. Isolation has served its purpose. Absorbing what is right, and discarding what is wrong, has enabled the hermit to learn the lessons of life. Now his vision is clear, and his mind is untroubled. He can approach new undertakings with confidence.

One who has laboured to improve themselves in this way can proceed with true authority. They will command widespread respect.

He is like the prince, who after preparation and study, is fit to accept the throne of his father.

Summary

A situation has reached a point where the past will serve to build the future. Existing circumstances ('the hermitage') can be left behind with the assurance that what lies ahead is progress. The lessons of life, which include past failures and successes, will all play their part. Experience is the keyword here; the ability to look at developments and assess their merit based on known precedents. This qualified approach will lead the way to a successful conclusion. The image of the prince accepting the throne of his father is a familiar story of progression through achievement. It is true authority, or a superior position, earned by an intrinsic right.

Conclusion

Jupiter in Virgo indicates the tendency to assess matters with a critical eye. The star sign's corresponding Tarot card, trump IX, The Hermit, means a need for isolation or withdrawal, discretion, illumination from within. On the Tree of Life the star sign and trump occupy the path between Sun and Jupiter. With the entry of Jupiter into the world of the trump it means that all the elements are in the right place; there is no imbalance, conflict or obstacles. The contemplative hermit can leave the hermitage, for the appearance of Jupiter signals a goal achieved. It is the water of Jupiter bringing life to the still earth of Virgo.

5 in 7

5= Mars, 7= the star sign Libra and Tarot trump VIII, Adjustment. Mars rules the element fire, Libra is of air.

Willing Acceptance

The scales are in balance, the objective is won. Yet there is argument and strife.

When the strife was not foreseen, the objective was foolish. If the strife was foreseen it was accepted as a passing phase, a stage on the path to improvement. It is beyond this stage of strife that one must look for the true objective.

To be prepared for strife, to accept it willingly, the true objective must be highly valued. Then the strife is met with a fighting spirit, and the conflict engaged with passion.

Those who willingly encounter strife must look beyond the trials of the moment. The fighting spirit knows a contest as an ugly wall to be broken; it is a barrier to overcome before liberating goodness.

Goodness, not strife, inspires a warrior.

Summary

This is a clear indication that the way ahead consists of two stages; a conflict of interests preceding the acquisition of the final goal. The oracle lays it on the line: go this way only if there is enough determination to overcome resistance. The passage opens by saying that the scales are in balance. This means that everything is in order; there is nothing to suggest a wrong move. The resistance is part and parcel of what lies ahead. It cannot be avoided. The key is in the closing paragraph, where there is a reminder to 'look beyond the trials of the moment'. This is because the resistance is a temporary phase, and what should be kept in mind is the 'goodness' – or the attraction of the goal – as providing sufficient motivation to press on.

Conclusion

Mars in Libra indicates a tendency to be argumentative. The star sign's corresponding Tarot card, trump VIII, Adjustment, means treaties, the formation of partnerships, marriage and vindication of truth. On the Tree of Life the star sign and trump occupy the path between Sun and Mars. The intrusion of Mars into the world of the trump suggests a goal accomplished – but the sphere of Mars is one of the most difficult to encounter. The fiery and war-like forces of disruption need careful handling. What it means in this case is that those forces will be engaged knowingly, and one must be prepared to deal with the consequences. Returning the aggression will not win the day. Absorbing it without any submission, while aiming for something higher and better, is the way forward and up. It is the fire of Mars heating but not destabilizing the calm air of Libra.

6 in 8

6= Sun, 8= the star sign Scorpio and Tarot trump XIII, Death. Sun rules the element air, Scorpio is of water.

Respite

The harvest is gathered. The harvester lays down his scythe, knowing that all is well.

He looks to the crop and sees a plentiful harvest. To either side are weeds and brambles, cut, gathered up and separated from the crop. He has acted with diligence and positioned everything in its due place. There is no inaccuracy in his labour.

With the harvest gathered there is a time of respite. His scythe can rest, with its edge resharpened.

Now is not the time for sowing, but for enjoying the fruits of the harvest. When the harvester acts with diligence, he knows in advance that respite draws closer.

Summary

This is a case where correct actions have produced a successful result. The harvest is a symbol of reward, the payment for past endeavours. The weeds and brambles are superfluous or obstructive matters which have been dealt with correctly and rendered harmless. They cannot stand in the way or spoil the main harvest. The scythe that can rest is the means and efforts employed to achieve this position; blunted by use, this valuable tool is due for resharpening to serve once again. But that time of service is not now, nor is it the time for sowing, or the laying down of plans for future actions. A goal has been achieved; it is time to enjoy the benefits of that goal.

Conclusion

Sun in Scorpio indicates the desire to make changes to create improved conditions. The star sign's corresponding Tarot card, trump XIII, Death, means starting afresh, unexpected change, transformation. (Please note that the card does *not* mean or imply physical death.) On the Tree of Life the star sign and trump occupy the path between Venus and Sun. The current appearance of Sun in the world of the trump signifies a goal accomplished for the Tarot character. The title of the Sun's sphere is Beauty, an apt name for a zone of balance and harmony. These are qualities which will manifest as the result of past actions. It is the air of Sun injecting new breath into the darkling waters of Scorpio.

7 in 9

7= Venus, 9= the star sign Sagittarius and Tarot trump XIV, Art.
Venus rules the element fire, Sagittarius is of fire.

The Cauldron

Blending in the cauldron, and producing something of value, is like the act of primal creation. The mix must be balanced, so that one ingredient does not overwhelm all the rest. This is how the universe survives; balance ensures a steady existence. Yet even here, in the universe, the seeds of decay are sown. When time wears thin all movement will cease. We exist temporarily and by the grace of equilibrium. The lessons of the years are there to read; it is foolish to speed the ending of time.

When the cauldron is filled without due care, nothing of value will emerge. Time and effort are wasted. Waste encourages the seeds of decay. Decay speeds the ending of a moment in time.

No matter how small the cauldron, it is like the act of primal creation. It must be tended with devotion.

Summary

Some oracles are distinctly mystical in tone, and they are always the result of processes which exist mainly in realms beyond the physical world. Thought is one such example. Thought is so nebulous in structure and origin that some scientists have questioned whether it has any connection with the physical brain – as nonsensical as that may sound. This oracle is a prime example of thought processes going awry. Care and attention are the end products of controlled thought, and not enough 'devotion' has been given to an act of creation. The cauldron is an image of a method of working; it is the technique, tools, ways and means all rolled into one, and it is currently in the hands of someone who has allowed their vision to be clouded or diverted. They have failed to see things for what they are, and in consequence 'nothing of value will emerge'.

Conclusion

Venus in Sagittarius indicates a tendency to be superficial and to avoid commitments. The star sign's corresponding Tarot card, trump XIV, Art, means the joining of forces, harmonious partnerships, control of volatile situations. Venus entering the world of this Tarot character is not conducive to any of those meanings. On the Tree of Life, the star sign and trump occupy a path on the important middle pillar. Venus is a step to one side; it is a diversion, and the negative aspects of that planet hold sway. Envy, greed and self-indulgence are examples to provide a feel for the darker side of Venus, although none of those instances may actually apply in this case. It is the negative current, rather than a variety of specifics, that is relevant. An error of judgement, most likely through an incomplete understanding of all the factors involved, will see the contents of this particular cauldron fail.

8 in 10

8= Mercury, 10= the star sign Capricorn and Tarot trump XV, The Devil. Mercury rules the element air, Capricorn is of earth.

Begin the Ascent

The mountain goat stands at the foot of the mountain. He is ready to make the ascent, keen to rise to the heights. He scrutinizes the path, the rocks, the vegetation. He sniffs the wind and tests for rain. He eyes his cloven hoofs and considers their strength, their grip. And so he continues with his thoughtful preparations.

The mountain goat is being untrue to his nature.

He is an efficient wild beast; his normal conduct is to roam without restraint, to act as instinct demands in the heat of the moment. In the most hostile environment, he is steady and firm. To spend his time in thoughtful preparation will not change the mountain's challenge. His moments must be taken as they come.

He is in the correct place, and he knows the mountain well. Let him begin the ascent and hold true to his instinct.

Summary

This oracle has nothing to do with indecision or uncertainty. The fault is a needless appraisal of external matters which are detracting from the core issue. The mountain is the intended goal, and it is a known quantity. There is no reason to hold back on the basis that the unexpected might happen, for the unexpected almost certainly will happen at some stage. That is the utterly random, chaotic nature of life. The only question of importance concerns the goal itself. 'He is in the right place, and he knows the mountain well' is the one proviso that counts. If the goal is understood to be comfortably within reach, and appears as free as can be expected of any sense of danger, then there are no grounds for self-doubt. 'His moments must be taken as they come' is an indication that nothing is likely to surface that will create an impassable barrier. All that is needed is the conviction to proceed.

Conclusion

Mercury in Capricorn signifies a serious approach which can override a creative imagination. Capricorn's associated Tarot card, trump XV, The Devil, means hidden forces at work, secret activities, unscrupulous methods. On the Tree of Life, the sign and trump occupy the path between Mercury and Sun. The entrance of Mercury into the world of the Tarot character means that everything is in the right place, and the character is extremely well placed to advance. He is exactly where he should be. The difficulty is that Mercury is holding a dominant position, and while this is no bad thing in the main (it is, after all, a sign that nothing is in conflict) it will have the effect of creating worries, theories, considerations – a whole spectrum of thought processes – to rise up like meddling phantoms. Mercury can be a trickster, and in this instance that is how it manifests its actions. Treat them for what they are.

9 in 11

9= Luna, 11= the star sign Aquarius and Tarot trump XVII, The Star. Luna rules the element air, Aquarius is of air.

No Reward

The light from a star is unchanging through the centuries. It is stable and reliable. The light of our day, the bringer of life, is starlight. Our Sun is a star, stable, reliable. The darkness of our night is the world turning; even in the dead of night we know daylight will return. Stability is constancy. To favour the moonlight, to favour endless change, brings no reward to those who need constancy.

There are those who are as constant as a star. They are admired by all, they can be trusted. There are those who wax and wane; they change from fullness to absence. They have few admirers. They are like ants, moving above the stones, beneath the stones, in the garden of life.

When a star becomes a moon, it is a time for mourning.

Summary

The message here is a clear warning. A potential for good is being undermined by an uncharacteristic wavering of attitude. It is a fault that introduces uncertainty. The key is in the last line, 'When a star becomes a moon, it is a time for mourning'. This means that the constancy and sheer dependability of a star did once exist, but has now been lost. The first sentence reminds us, 'The light from a star is unchanging through the centuries', therefore that same light or dependable trait must still exist, but its flow is being interrupted or blocked in some way. The strength of reason for that interruption or blockage will mark the duration of this sorry state of affairs. This can apply equally to an individual, to a once promising situation or to a larger group, as when, for example, an established company begins to flounder.

Conclusion

Luna in Aquarius indicates a desire to expand social contacts. The Tarot card corresponding with Aquarius, trump XVII, The Star, means the expansion of horizons, increased vigour, a new outlook. Luna entering the world of that trump has a damaging effect. On the Tree of Life the trump occupies a high and advanced path, while the sphere of Luna is much further down the scale. This combination represents a retrograde step without any saving graces. In its negative aspect, Luna is the bringer of illusion and deception, and these are the forces at work here. The inherent clarity of The Star character is thrown out of true as a result, although she is perfectly capable of restoring herself given adequate time. Luna's effects are temporary more often than not, but while they last they can be deeply disturbing. It is the air of Luna and the air of Aquarius combining in a windstorm.

3 in 12

3= Saturn, 12= the star sign Pisces and Tarot trump XVIII, The Moon. Saturn rules the element water, Pisces is of water.

Jackals

The sun flames down on the desert. Nothing grows in this arid place. The winds move the sands, changing the look of the land so that no mark is familiar. Jackals prowl, hungry and thirsty.

For jackals to survive they must have nourishment. They must eat and drink. This desert is not their home; it is not the place where food and water exist together. What they look for is fallen prey, so that no effort is spent in a lengthy pursuit. When they have found their meal they will feast, and then return to their places of comfort.

The desert is vast. To cross it one must have adequate provisions. To step beneath the sun without due preparation is to nourish the jackals.

Summary

The desert is a hostile environment, representing a situation containing nothing but hardship and danger. The sands are moving daily so that everything changes; there is a constant shifting of an unsteady base. The jackals are hunters, preying on the weak and exposed. When they have had their fill they will leave. They will thrive but the fallen will not.

It is a question of advance preparation. The ship of the desert, the camel, is famous for its endurance and it survives because it has all it needs before it sets out. The decision must be taken in advance: if the journey is worth it, prepare accordingly. Like the camel, there is a way to win through. If hardship and danger are not worth the risk, do not take one step.

Conclusion

Saturn in Pisces indicates a lack of organization. The star sign's corresponding Tarot card, trump XVIII, The Moon, means illusion, deceit, a crisis of faith, the brink. Saturn is highly placed on the Tree of Life, whereas the sign and trump share a path at the very base. The gulf between them is too great for Saturn to bestow any benefits. Instead, it delivers a 'keep back' warning. The darker side of Saturn takes over, bringing restriction and decline to a trump already gloomy in nature. There is a ray of light in that Saturn can impose control, which would be of advantage where 'jackals' are concerned. The oracle is not about chaos but a steady running down and erosion – hence the image of the desert. Saturn is slow to move; there is enough time and opportunity to prepare and to restore command. It must ultimately depend on whether the end will justify the means.

4 in 1

4= Jupiter, 1= the star sign Aries and Tarot trump IV, The Emperor. Jupiter rules the element water, Aries is of fire.

Careful Husbandry

The emperor stands in a benevolent mood. He sees wealth all around him in the palace, and vows to share his abundance with the needy of his empire. There will be happiness in humble quarters.

When all the wealth is spent, the emperor will know that he has only himself to give. The needy will have tasted luxury; they will not give up their benefits. They will turn against their benevolent emperor.

Lasting prosperity throughout the empire is maintained by careful husbandry. Sharing and dividing should not exceed reasonable limits. Grain must always be found in the store house for planting.

Summary

The emperor is a source of support, and need not necessarily refer to a person. This support is not as stable as it might appear on the surface, although there is no malicious intention to deceive. If anything it suggests a desire to give too much, when it is not prudent to do so. It is a lesson in the management of affairs and resources. There is inadequate provision for long term stability, and through that failing matters will eventually come to a head.

Conclusion

Jupiter in Aries indicates an expansive approach, a need to widen existing limits. The star sign's corresponding Tarot card, trump IV, The Emperor, means vigour, aspiration, rule and conquest. The emperor is a relatively unstable character, for in astrology Aries is the first appearance of the fire element. It is the outpouring of fierce flame, which although controlled to a certain point is far from steady. It sears and scorches from a distance with its swift creative energy. Jupiter entering the emperor's world has the effect that the planet most often delivers; a sense of grandness and magnificence. On the Tree of Life it is a little too far above the path of the trump for the emperor to accommodate safely. The stabilizing effects of Jupiter are lost in an inflated furnace. It is the water of Jupiter simmering before the untamed fire of Aries.

5 in 2

5= Mars, 2= the star sign Taurus and Tarot trump V, The Hierophant. Mars rules the element fire, Taurus is of earth.

Two Friends

Patience and composure are two friends of the student. When the student is engaged in vigorous activity, with mind and spirit distracted, little is learned. It is worse by far when the teacher, not the student, is at fault. The two friends are vital to a teacher. A teacher's responsibilities should not be forgotten; impetuous actions will produce harmful errors. The companion of error is grief.

Teaching is best carried out by example. Thus we are all teachers. The examples we set are seen by others; what they see teaches them about us, about our world.

When a teacher is seen to act rashly, students withdraw. They do not value a person with a world that is reckless. No person from such a world has ever risen to prominence.

Summary

This oracle speaks of a teacher as being a person, although it could possibly refer to an important source of guidance or support. What is clear is that this help is on the wane. Energy is at work that does not belong; instead of informing and helping it is dispersing. The 'students' of the oracle are those who rely on the teacher. They are accustomed to an established routine or way of working, and now they can see negative changes taking place. They will withdraw, that is disassociate themselves and keep their distance, rather than be seen as a source of encouragement.

Conclusion

Mars in Taurus indicates a potential for self-destruction through carelessness. The star sign's corresponding Tarot card, trump V, The Hierophant, means stubborn strength, toil, teaching, goodness of heart. On the Tree of Life the sign and trump occupy a path above the sphere of Mars. The entry of Mars into the world of the trump is therefore a backward step, and one not helped by the fiery nature of the planet. Mars is conflict and furious energy, characteristics which have no rightful place in the Hierophant's domain. The character became a teacher with goodness of heart by dint of concerted effort and sacrifice. To allow the effects of Mars to linger will be a serious error. It is the fire of Mars agitating the deep earth of Taurus.

6 in 3

6= Sun, 3= the star sign Gemini and Tarot trump VI, The Lovers. Sun rules the element air, Gemini is of air.

New Ground

Turning their back on sunlight, the lovers walk together towards darkness.

A position of value is not left for the sake of a minor incentive. The lovers are shrewd. They know when to stand still and when to go forward. They know when to reject familiar habits, and when it is time to break new ground.

In sunlight we have vision, in darkness we are blind. The lovers used their time in sunlight to advantage. They planned their way to enter the dark and break new ground. They used their vision by day to understand the darkness of night.

The lovers are shrewd. They will not fail.

Summary

The lovers can be two people, or one person carrying their desired ambition in their heart. The darkness has several meanings. On one level it represents the unknown future; on another it is the obstacles and trials they will encounter. But the lovers are shrewd, for they signify a high degree of achievement. By assessing the known, they can calculate the risks of the unknown. Those risks are seen as manageable. It is as clear a sign of encouragement as they could wish for that their plans are viable and worth putting into practice.

Conclusion

Sun in Gemini indicates a desire to pursue self-expression. Gemini's corresponding Tarot card, trump VI, The Lovers, means intuition, intelligence and swift adaptability. On the Tree of Life the sign and trump occupy an important path from Sun to Saturn. The appearance of Sun in the world of the trump demonstrates that all is as it should be. There is no conflict, and the Tarot characters are soundly based. They have the perfect starting point. That starting point is the sunlight of the oracle on which the lovers turn their backs. They are not ignoring our Sun; they are moving away from it to a higher elevation. This journey takes them to Saturn, which is across the abyss and is the penultimate meaning of the darkness they walk towards. It is the gulf that divides the upper realms of the ideal, or spirit, from the lower worlds of progressive manifestation. It is a gulf that cannot be crossed carrying baggage from the past. The lovers approach this gulf willingly and in the full knowledge of the sacrifices they must make. What they gain will far exceed their losses. In a purely materialistic sense it means new horizons at the end of a planned escape from outmoded routines. It is the air of Sun embracing the air of Gemini.

7 in 4

7= Venus, 4= the star sign Cancer and Tarot trump VII, The Chariot. Venus rules the element fire, Cancer is of water.

Remain Loyal

The charioteer was accepted into the ranks of the army. It is his duty to accept the will of his high command.

The charioteer will remember that the army is of his own free choosing. They in turn have placed in him their highest faith. His instructions and orders must be accepted without question. Important tasks are not given to those unfit to perform them.

There can be no turning back for the charioteer. He must remain loyal to his army. To abandon one cause for the sake of another will not bring approval. Great leaders do not admire the capricious or the weak.

Orders of importance are rarely accepted without some trepidation. The charioteer will succeed if he adheres to what is right.

Summary

The charioteer can be male or female; they are the person who is the main driving force, while the army is a symbol for an individual, group or goal with a major influence on the charioteer's life. In a higher sense the army is also an emblem of a personal, deeply held and impelling conviction. Little so far has transpired to shatter that conviction. The fault is with the charioteer, who is experiencing an unsettling doubt arising from the validity of choices made or actions taken in the past. The oracle is stating in so many words that those choices or actions were correct and binding, for 'There can be no turning back'. An important issue has surfaced and given rise to anxiety, but the charioteer is a central and powerful figure with ample reserves to succeed.

Conclusion

Venus in Cancer indicates a tendency to be sentimental, with a detrimental effect on level thinking. Cancer's corresponding Tarot card, trump VII, The Chariot, means success through initiative, the surmounting of obstacles, victory through effort. The sign and trump occupy an elevated path on the Tree of Life, far above the sphere of Venus. The entry of Venus into the world of the charioteer is a distinctly backward step, even though that planet has less damaging effects on other Tarot characters existing at a similar level. There is no sympathy between the trump and Venus, no hidden link to act as a buffer. The result is that the charioteer is temporarily wrong-footed, assailed by the negative influences of that planet which include greed, envy and disloyalty. It should not be long before the charioteer has a firm grip on the reins once again. It is the fire of Venus retreating before the rushing water of Cancer.

8 in 5

8= Mercury, 5= the star sign Leo and Tarot trump XI, Lust. Mercury rules the element water, Leo is of fire.

Shut and Open

The woman is in two minds. She is not her customary self. She is known for her balanced approach, her sharp vision that can search the dark and light and the facts they hold. She does not allow her strength to mask her weakness; she relies on one to contain the other, so that her decisions remain fair. Yet she is in two minds. She is being unreasonable.

The light will overwhelm the dark, the dark will retaliate.

Weakness can train a savage lion; a savage lion can defend the weak. When either is being unreasonable they cannot stay in each other's company.

It is human nature to waver at times. But when one eye is deliberately shut and the other kept open, the lion will seize its chance.

Summary

This is not indecision or the inability to make a choice through lack of information; this is a form of obstinacy. When enough facts are known to reach a decision but that decision is avoided, it is usually through fear or dislike of the consequences. There is then a kind of internal tug-of-war, seeing both sides but reluctant to change the status quo. This approach is at best a temporary delay, for one day something will have to give way. The longer it is left, the more damage can be done: 'the lion will seize its chance'.

Conclusion

Mercury in Leo indicates a lack of objectivity, and an increase in self-expression. Leo's corresponding Tarot card, trump XI, Lust, means the reconciliation of opposing forces, the opportunity to advance, great courage. The sign and trump occupy a path on the Tree of Life between Mars and Jupiter, the opposing forces of strength and mercy respectively. The woman and lion characters of the trump illustrate those forces held in balance. The entry of Mercury into the world of the trump signals an imbalance, a wrong turn. As Mercury is dominantly a planet representing thought processes, it is in that specific area that the imbalance will show itself. The normal state of poise is disturbed. The trump has nothing to do with deception, therefore the disturbance will be more of a digging-in of heels, a refusal to accept what is plainly true. It does not bode well for the happy union of woman and lion, which can be two people or one person and their desired aims. As they are fundamentally a pair the disturbance should be eradicated. It is the air of Mercury scattering the earth of Leo.

9 in 6

9= Luna, 6= the star sign Virgo and Tarot trump IX, The Hermit. Luna rules the element air, Virgo is of earth.

The Glow

The hermit closes the door to the hermitage, sealing himself in. There is light from the window. He closes the blinds.

On the table is his lamp, with the light that never dies. He turns up the light, bathing in its glow.

Seated quietly, the hermit begins his meditation.

The world outside continues to turn. There is activity and sound, advance and retreat, growth and decay, failure and success. People hurry on their business, children play. The world is busy, the world is alive.

Through his eyelids, the hermit sees the glow from his lamp.

Summary

It is a time for withdrawal, rather than action. Circumstances do not warrant anything other than taking time out. That time should be used constructively, in an assessment of needs and ambitions, and a review of the practicalities of life. As the oracle illustrates, there is a personal ideal due for consideration. Internally the hermit is reaching for his soul, aware that some things are eternal and although unseen directly, are apparent in the way they filter through our lives. It is often the calm internal light that far outweighs all the substance of a hectic world. The message is that there is an internal truth of a kind, a deeply held conviction that must be allowed to remain intact at this time. It is rather like getting one's batteries charged, rather than expending effort.

Conclusion

Luna in Virgo indicates a tendency to be practical and methodical. Virgo's corresponding Tarot card, trump IX, The Hermit, means withdrawal from current events, illumination from within, discretion, careful planning. The sign and trump occupy a path on the Tree of Life higher than the sphere of Luna. The entrance of Luna should indicate a retrograde step, which it does but in a curiously helpful way. The paths are processes of change and activity; Luna has the effect of negating that activity for the hermit by stimulating visionary qualities. This hermit in real life is no recluse; it is what they carry in their hearts and minds that distinguish them. Visionary qualities are no drawback in this case. They are a positive benefit when it comes to evaluating core principles.

3 in 7

3= Saturn, 7= the star sign Libra and Tarot trump VIII, Adjustment. Saturn rules the element water, Libra is of air.

Reunion

The bride and groom have travelled far. From humble beginnings they grew in status, always as friends yet to meet. They passed through adversity and the black days of doubt, wishing for comfort from the unknown friend. Yet they never looked back. Fear looks back; hope looks forward.

An unknown friend is like a missing limb. The body is incomplete; day by day it knows a part of the whole is absent. Even the body senses an unknown friend.

When paths converge and the two meet at last, it is more than a first meeting. It is a reunion.

Such friends shall become bride and groom. It is destiny.

Summary

A situation long in the making is about to reach its culmination. The oracle speaks of a bride and groom, not husband and wife; therefore there is a final step to go. But that is a technicality. The real work has been done and the union will take place. The bride and groom may be two people or one person and their cherished plan. Their 'humble beginnings' refer more to their learning curves than to considerations of wealth. The whole tone of the oracle is positive; it tells of progressive growth from a small start to a point where there is every right to expect fulfillment. The two friends 'yet to meet' is a way of expressing a feeling of something meant to be. Whether or not you believe in destiny, there are many cases where a particular end is inevitable.

Conclusion

Saturn in Libra indicates a good sense of time and place, plus the skills to achieve an end. Libra's corresponding Tarot card, trump VIII, Adjustment, means treaties, the formation of partnerships, the vindication of truth. The sign and trump occupy a path on the Tree of Life between Sun and Mars, indicating beauty and strength respectively. The entrance of Saturn is a jump ahead to a loftier realm, which for the trump is an advantage. Adjustment was a trump called Justice in the old packs, but as the author of the improved version pointed out, '...it is not to be considered as one of the facts of Nature. Nature is not just ... but Nature is exact.'[1] The heart of this trump is one of staying true to nature and maintaining adjustment of disorder by natural balance, for which the planet Saturn is an ideal assistant. In its positive aspect Saturn brings order and control, yet there is much about it that connects with feminine insight. Saturn's sphere on the Tree is called Understanding, a positive contribution to the art of creating balance and in turn, harmony. It is the water of Saturn supporting the air of Libra, as the oceans support the sky.

1 Aleister Crowley.

4 in 8

4= Jupiter, 8= the star sign Scorpio and Tarot trump XIII, Death. Jupiter rules the element water, Scorpio is of water.

Cutting Down

Carelessness with a reaper's scythe brings sorrow and bitter regret. A fine harvest is gathered from a fine crop. When a fine crop is gathered along with weeds, the reaper has failed to exercise caution. The mixed harvest will find no customer.

A good scythe is a potent tool. It is easy for exhilaration to lead the way, to see the blade sweeping with power and efficiency. Cutting down becomes a joy. The greater the joy, the greater the final desolation.

The reaper and his scythe proceed in error. A fine harvest will serve many, a mixed harvest will serve none. The reaper himself will go hungry. His obligation is to provide for those in his care. Through carelessness he will end by taking away.

Summary

'Cutting down' is really a process of selection, or should be. It is working towards a personal advantage while dismissing anything seen as unhelpful. Cutting down, harvesting and retaining on the one hand, weeding out on the other. It is obviously sensible to cut down and gather things of value, but foolish to include anything contrary. The key is in the words, 'it is easy for exhilaration to lead the way'. Motivated by the impression that the chosen course is beyond criticism, or destined to succeed beyond any doubt, it is a short step from there to acting without regard for obvious pitfalls.

Conclusion

Jupiter in Scorpio indicates the desire to gain power and control over people and situations. Scorpio's corresponding Tarot card, trump XIII, Death, means starting afresh, unexpected change, transformation. (Note that it does not mean or imply physical death. It refers only to a process of change.) On the Tree of Life the sign and trump occupy a path between Venus and Sun, signifying victory and beauty respectively. The entrance of Jupiter into the world of the trump is a step ahead. For many Tarot characters this would be an advantage, but this trump is overwhelmed by the majesty of Jupiter. The last thing any wielder of a scythe needs is Jupiter's sense of expansive majesty. What they really need is concentration and control. With a misguided conviction that their actions are based on secure foundations, they plunge forward without care. Everything is acceptable. It is the water of Jupiter joining with the water of Scorpio in a destructive flood.

5 in 9

5= Mars, 9= the star sign Sagittarius and Tarot trump XIV, Art. Mars rules the element fire, Sagittarius is of fire.

The Servant

The woman with the cauldron would do well not to light the fire. She has heat enough in her heart without adding flame to flame. Yet the potion is mixed, and it warms by itself.

Warming without fire is an indication of ingredients that fight. The powders do not blend; they react with ferocity.

Steam rising when no fire is lit is a warning. If the woman's heart is still responding, she will see the steam and start afresh. If she sees it but expresses joy, she will lose everything of value.

Those who create marvellous works may see flame as a useful servant. When the servant takes command it is not a sign of success. It is defeat at the hands of our oldest enemy.

Summary

Our oldest enemy and our oldest friend; fire. In this case it is not the crackling flame, but the heat of something equally creative or destructive – passion. The passion that stems from a mind in tumult, a mind beset with doubts and fears and in danger of meltdown. It is not rage directed at a specific target, more a case of a general and burning feeling of impotence. Circumstances are almost out of control. Without any apparent reason there are obstacles and irritations rising of their own accord, '…the potion is mixed, and it warms by itself'. The warnings of conflict are there but if interpreted as a form of revenge to be imposed on others, it will not go as planned. Starting again with a more detached and cooler approach is the better and safer option.

Conclusion

Mars in Sagittarius indicates the tendency to try for objectives beyond reach. The star sign's corresponding Tarot card, trump XIV, Art, means the joining of forces, harmonious partnerships, control of volatile situations, success. All those meanings are laid to waste by the entrance of Mars into the world of the trump. On the Tree of Life the sign and trump occupy a path on the middle pillar – an important location, with a direct line to the high realms of spirit. Mars is away to one side and presents a distraction. Moreover the negative forces of the planet take over; imbalance, disruption, fury and ultimately, destruction. The Tarot character will not suffer permanently for she is too enduring and resilient. But no time should be lost in returning to the straight and narrow.

6 in 10

6= Sun, 10= the star sign Capricorn and Tarot trump XV, The Devil. Sun rules the element air, Capricorn is of earth.

Spring

In the midst of summer the sun is high and the earth is warmed. The days are long, the people content. In the midst of summer, the long days of joy reach their end.

The sun turns south in the midst of summer. Climbing to lesser heights in the midday sky, sunlight lessens and the days grow shorter. Slowly, progressively, in the midst of summer winter comes.

On the darkest day of winter, summer comes. The sun turns north. The days grow longer and the sun climbs higher in the midday sky. On the darkest day of winter it is time to prepare for the celebrations of spring.

To know the seasons is to know when to prepare. From the longest day the days grow short, from the shortest day the days grow long. The longest day of summer is an omen for regret. The shortest, coldest day of winter is a jewel.

Summary

This is a reminder of the natural course of the seasons, and how our own fortunes follow the celestial tides of change. It may not be the 'darkest day of winter' for the current situation, but it is a lesson that life is rarely as it seems. When there appears to be a bleak outlook with no hope in sight, something comes along and turns the tables. The last line of the oracle has the most significance, for it draws attention to the fact that the 'shortest, coldest day' is a jewel. This day can occur in a personal sense at any time of year, as it speaks of an emotional viewpoint rather than a reference to climate. As a closing statement it sums up the oracle's optimistic and encouraging outlook, for earlier it says of this day, '...it is time to prepare for the celebrations of spring'.

Conclusion

Sun in Capricorn indicates a desire to take control and take nothing for granted. Capricorn's corresponding Tarot card, trump XV, The Devil, means hidden forces at work, secret activities, unscrupulous methods. On the Tree of Life the sign and trump occupy the path between Mercury and Sun, representing glory and beauty respectively. Not only does the appearance of Sun in the Tarot character's world mean that all things are in order, more importantly it signifies a goal accomplished. In astrology, Capricorn is the sign in which the sun ends its winter southbound journey and heads north once again. Hence the oracle's enthusiastic references to spring, reminding us of the benefits those inspirational months freely bring. It is the air of Sun permeating and uplifting the earth of Capricorn.

7 in 11

7= Venus, 11= the star sign Aquarius and Tarot trump XVII, The Star. Venus rules the element fire, Aquarius is of air.

Filling a Jug

To empty water from one jug into another, one must be confident that the lower jug can hold all the contents of the higher. If the lower jug is too small, the water will spill over. The lost water is then a sign of imprudence or overconfidence.

It is imprudent not to consider the size of the jug, but to proceed regardless. This is wasteful of valuable resources. When the jug is at hand and plainly visible, to ignore its limitations is to invite loss.

Overconfidence is assessing the jug without care and attention. Deciding it is suitable merely because it is attractive gives confidence when none is due.

Filling a jug is a simple act. The rules of filling hide abundant lessons.

Summary

Our perception of what is right or wrong, achievable or beyond reach, can never be based on subjective reasoning alone. Facts must speak for themselves and they must form part of the choices we make. The difficulty is in discovering those facts on the one hand, and accepting them on the other. Life is rarely simple and most situations go deeper than they appear. Extracting facts can take time, and we need to ask the right questions, look in the right places. Once we have all the necessary information, we may not like what we see. Nonetheless, we must recognize the reality and modify our choices accordingly. The alternative is to pay for a mistake.

Conclusion

Venus in Aquarius indicates a tendency to be drawn towards eccentric or unconventional pursuits. The star sign's corresponding Tarot card, trump XVII, The Star, means the expansion of horizons, increased vigour, new outlook. On the Tree of Life the sign and trump occupy a high path between the spheres of Sun and Neptune, considerably above that of Venus. There are links between the trump and Venus, as indicated by the seven-pointed star within the trump's design – seven being the number of the planet. However those links do not stop the positive aspects of Venus (primarily love) from influencing the Tarot character in a negative way. The Star is filled with the glow of Venus, overbalancing her essential clarity of mind. She is flowing with idealistic impulses and visions, which filter through as a sense of overconfidence in her abilities. Her rosy view fails to accommodate stark reality. It is the fire of Venus expanding the air of Aquarius beyond acceptable limits.

8 in 12

8= Mercury, 12= the star sign Pisces and Tarot trump XVIII, The Moon. Mercury rules the element air, Pisces is of water.

Brother and Sister

The moon forever changes in appearance. In its nightly variations the moon is constant. For the moon, change reveals its steadiness. If the moon should stay full without waning, the permanence would show instability. It would threaten oceans and the world. The moon demonstrates its stability by the changes it makes.

When a mind does not know itself there is change. But the mind is not the moon. A mind that changes by day or night is not dependable.

The mind and the moon have sides we never see. The moon's hidden side is mountainous and dark; the mind's hidden side has its own mountains and darkness. The mind and the moon are like brother and sister. Both can shed light, both can delude.

A changing moon sheds its light on the world; a changing mind has only shadows to share.

Summary

A situation of confusion arises from a lack of permanence, and it is not only a mind that changes here. There is the tendency for circumstances to merge and flow in a bewildering stream, so that nothing appears to stay true for long. Reliability is almost entirely absent. This translates into the oracle's central theme of indecision, the inability to make a choice or form a realistic sense of direction. This is not mere dithering; it is a state approaching panic. Remember that this is an indication of future trends related to a particular question; the next step should be to ask how to avoid this negative outcome.

Conclusion

Mercury in Pisces indicates the tendency for a rational mind to be oversensitive, even cloudy and uncertain. The star sign's corresponding Tarot card, trump XVIII, The Moon, means illusion, deception, crisis, "the darkest hour before the dawn". On the Tree of Life the sign and trump occupy a low path leading from the sphere of Earth to Venus, called The Kingdom and Victory respectively. Mercury is a step up, which for other trumps could be a welcome move, but Mercury entering the gloomy world of this trump has damaging consequences. Mercury is attempting to introduce logic in a place where logic cannot exist. The result is a kind of short-circuit, reflecting in the outer world as a state of disorder. It is the air of Mercury lifting the water of Pisces into spray.

9 in 1

9= Luna, 1= the star sign Aries and Tarot trump IV, The Emperor. Luna rules the element air, Aries is of fire.

The New Road

The emperor is set to leave on a journey. His retinue waits, while he sits at ease with his daydreams.

The journey is a new venture. It is a new road leading to unexplored places. The emperor is rooted in tradition; he is fond of the established and the known. The obscurity of unknown places stirs his imagination; from imagination he passes into daydreams.

His advisors remind him that time presses. The emperor knows that dreams are false; whatever he sees will be a play of fancy. Though they keep him spellbound he must dismiss his whimsical thoughts.

The retinue prepares as the emperor takes his lead. They leave the palace gates and the dreams behind. It is a long road ahead, but a good road.

Summary

Taking that road is the only way the emperor will discover the worthwhile nature of the journey and its end. A journey into the unknown is a worrying experience, disturbing enough to create imaginary fears. But the whole world of the emperor is one of energy and conquest. It would be out of keeping with his nature to begin a journey if there was a probability it would fail. He is a symbol of inspired action, and while he may be stubborn and quarrelsome it is simply to achieve his ambitions. Doubts and fears in the face of the unknown are perfectly normal. The emperor will suffer them like anyone else, but he will not allow them to stand in his way – especially when the journey will end in triumph. There is no time like the present, which is why his advisors remind him 'that time presses'.

Conclusion

Luna in Aries indicates a tendency to experience abrupt waves of emotion. The star sign's corresponding Tarot card, trump IV, The Emperor, means aspiration, rule and conquest, originality. On the Tree of Life the sign and trump occupy a path between the spheres of Moon and Venus, called Foundation and Victory respectively. The entry of Luna into the world of the Tarot character means that everything is in order. There is no imbalance, no conflict. It is his correct starting point for the journey to Victory. The danger is that the emperor can be volatile and blustery. Luna will easily grip him with illusory visions and doubts; it is his task to overcome them, and he is stubborn enough to succeed. It is the air of Luna agitating the fire of Aries.

3 in 2

3= Saturn, 2= the star sign Taurus and Tarot trump V, The Hierophant. Saturn rules the element water, Taurus is of earth.

The Abyss

The wise teacher is standing on the brink of an abyss. If he looks behind he can see where he has been. Even with the abyss before him, he has no desire to retrace his steps.

If he looks down into the abyss he cannot see the bottom. The distance is too far, the shadow too deep.

When he looks across the abyss he can see his journey's end. There, ahead, is the culmination of his life's work. But there is no bridge across the abyss.

To reach this stage in his life he sought help from superiors. Now he stands alone. All he has is his wisdom as a teacher. Without fear, he steps forward.

He walks without falling.

All his life, he has been teaching how to cross the abyss.

Summary

The wise teacher is a symbol for someone who has learned by experience, and are held in regard. That experience has brought them to this point, where everything they believe in is put to the test. The abyss is a terrifying image of an accident waiting to happen, a place where crossing without visible support seems out of the question. Yet the accident does not come about for experience has shown how to succeed. All the same, belief is one thing; trusting to that belief – or practicing what you preach – is entirely another. In this case belief stands the test. What at first appears as a potential fall concludes satisfactorily. The 'teacher' was right to stand by his experiences and convictions and apply them.

Conclusion

Saturn in Taurus indicates great strength and resolve. The star sign's corresponding Tarot card, trump V, The Hierophant, means stubborn strength, teaching, wise counsel, help from superiors. On the Tree of Life the sign and trump occupy a high path of spiritual awareness. They cross the abyss, which divides the world of pure spirit above from the realms of increasing manifestation below. The symbolism of this abyss translates, in the present case, as an apparent gulf between the desired aim and the available means of achievement. The entry of Saturn into the world of the Tarot character signifies a massive injection of understanding into the situation, together with firm control. These combine to reveal and instigate a way through. It is the water of Saturn elevating the earth of Taurus.

4 in 3

4= Jupiter, 3= the star sign Gemini and Tarot trump VI, The Lovers. Jupiter rules the element water, Gemini is of air.

The First Gifts

Professing their admiration for each other, the couple exchange gifts. Both are overwhelmed by the luxury they receive. He silently vows to exceed her gift; she silently vows to exceed his.

Time passes and again the couple exchange gifts. Once more they are overwhelmed; once more they make their silent vows.

Time passes and again the couple exchange gifts. They look at nothing else, talk of nothing else. They smile but part without their eyes meeting.

The couple can go no further. When the object is the centre of importance, the giver has lost sight of the original purpose.

Summary

The oracle describes an ambition thwarted by too little consideration for what is actually required. Somehow attention has been sidetracked from the original aim. The ways and means to achieve that aim have outgrown their importance; they are acting as barriers to the very goal they were meant to reach. Little by little, side issues have adopted unwarranted importance. It may be fear of failure; it may be a reluctance to take on responsibility. The issue is whether the original aim is still worth pursuing. If it is the solution is clear; stop beating about the bush. If the situation has changed and the original aim no longer has the same merit, then it is better to abandon the whole approach and look for another direction.

Conclusion

Jupiter in Gemini indicates a tendency to concentrate on external matters and past experiences. Gemini's corresponding Tarot card, trump VI, The Lovers, means intuition, intelligence, swift adaptability. On the Tree of Life the sign and trump occupy a path at odds with the sphere of mighty Jupiter. It is a step to one side, a place where the Tarot characters have no need to be. Jupiter is stability and the root of all abundance, with no discord about it. Yet when it enters the world of the Tarot characters it introduces a force with no benefit to them. They have other requirements on their minds, other needs to fulfill. Theirs is a pursuit of harmony, allowing them to rise as one to higher levels. Jupiter's weight is holding them back, making them look behind instead of forward. It is the water of Jupiter burdening the air of Gemini.

5 in 4

5= Mars, 4= the star sign Cancer and Tarot trump VII, The Chariot. Mars rules the element fire, Cancer is of water.

Providence

The charioteer carries a small treasure of priceless value. The treasure cannot be spent, only put to work. No one but the charioteer is fit to conduct it to its place of working.

His journey is short, the road straight. There is one bridge that he must cross before his journey's end.

The charioteer has no fear of failure. He will deliver the treasure to its rightful place, and the treasure will begin its work.

Charioteer, treasure and rightful place; when the three come together it is a time of providence. The journey's end will justify the journey.

Summary

The charioteer will most likely represent a person, although it may equally represent a collective venture, or other but similar means to an end. The small treasure cannot be spent for it is not money; it is an idea, a purpose or intention. The journey is short and straight because the ultimate aim is achievable; few obstacles will present themselves as the route has been thoroughly planned. There is one bridge on the way, yet a bridge is not a barrier. A bridge is a place of crossing, a means of transition. One has to choose whether or not to cross, but as the treasure is due to be delivered that decision appears to be a foregone conclusion. It is ambition achieving its objective.

Conclusion

Mars in Cancer indicates a tendency towards emotional intensity. Cancer's corresponding Tarot card, trump VII, The Chariot, means triumph, victory and hope, although sometimes it can imply ruthlessness. On the Tree of Life the sign and trump occupy a high path between the spheres of Mars and Saturn, called Strength and Understanding respectively. The appearance of Mars in the world of the trump means that everything is in order; Mars is the correct starting point for the Tarot character's climb to attainment. There is no imbalance and nothing is out of place. Part of that climb entails crossing a divide which separates the realms of spirit above from their decline into matter below. This is the inescapable 'bridge' the character must face, although as the Summary makes clear it will appear in the mundane world as a period of change. For most other trumps the fiery planet Mars is a negative influence, but the charioteer is depicted clad in armour. He is on home territory. For the sake of interest, the card shows him carrying a bowl with radiant contents. The bowl is the Holy Grail, which sums up the potency of this character, and explains the priceless treasure that cannot be spent. Its purpose is to inform and improve the world.

6 in 5

6= Sun, 5= the star sign Leo and Tarot trump XI, Lust.
Sun rules the element air, Leo is of fire.

Marriage

A mirror shows a reflection; whatever is before the mirror appears in the glass as its twin. Yet the reflection is not true to the original; the left has become right and the right has become left. The image people have of themselves is from the mirror they see every day. Other people see the true original, where left is left and right is right. The image people have of themselves is seen by no one. They do not exist.

Desire, need, ambition and intention; all these can be like a mirror image. They will never emerge beyond the world of imagination. Those who marry the image with reality see the image disappear. What remains is not embellished but it reveals what is possible.

Summary

Although it appears to have a slight warning tone this oracle is an encouragement. The mirror is a dividing line between the real world and the world of imagination. In that imaginary world it is all too easy to harbour ideas that do not connect with facts as they stand. It takes a determined mind to dismantle long-held misconceptions and reappraise cherished ideas. The world is full of possibilities. Some may not have had the attention they deserved; perhaps they were seen as beyond a favoured zone of interest. But once that favoured zone has been examined for its faults, the boundaries can be redrawn. They can be expanded to include hitherto impossible goals, which, because they are now perceived in a true light, are suddenly realised as possible.

Conclusion

Sun in Leo indicates a strong sense of enthusiasm and self-confidence. Leo's corresponding Tarot card, trump XI, Lust, means strength, courage, energy and action. On the Tree of Life the sign and trump occupy the path between the spheres of Mars and Jupiter, called Strength and Mercy respectively. This path is above the Sun sphere, which suggests a slight backward step when that planet enters the world of the trump. Slight, because the sphere is perfectly midway below the path of Leo and trump XI, almost like a point of balance on a pair of level scales. This, coupled with the fact that Sun creates harmony, brings a resurgence to the trump of the forces that first brought the Tarot characters together. It acts as a renewing energy, revitalizing the synthesis and analysis that makes harmony possible. Before harmony there is a process of shedding false appearances. What emerges is an honest union destined to go forward. It is the air of Sun giving life to the fire of Leo.

7 in 6

7= Venus, 6= the star sign Virgo and Tarot trump IX, The Hermit. Venus rules the element fire, Virgo is of earth.

The Pendulum

There are times when stillness is necessary. Like the swinging of a pendulum we move into action, then retreat to gather strength. We could not continue without gathering strength. Once we are strong, the way we move into action reveals the essence of who we are.

There are those who use movement and stillness to good effect. They employ a sense of balanced conduct in all they do. There are those who would deny stillness and favour movement. They make demanding companions. They object to what they see as weakness. Their essence is a burning fuse.

When life is too demanding, those who are sensible must retreat. They must withdraw to gather strength. It is not failure; it is a sign of their determination to succeed. They ensure the pendulum will always be restored. Their essence is commendable.

Summary

There are two issues at stake. The second paragraph speaks of a burning fuse, the early sign of a self-destruct catastrophe. There is a refusal to accept what is perfectly clear in theory, and a rebuttal of conditions as they stand in practice. It is a fixed resolve to plough on, seeing failures in others though none in themselves. The second issue deals with practicalities, the recognition of a correct approach. Ploughing on regardless is dismissed in favour of stepping back and reviewing tactics and direction. This revision is vital to success – although it may end in a direction not considered previously. The oracle regards this adaptability as commendable. Success cannot be treated with scorn.

Conclusion

Venus in Virgo indicates a tendency to be unduly critical. Virgo's corresponding Tarot card, trump IX, The Hermit, means illumination from within, the need for withdrawal or isolation, careful planning. On the Tree of Life the sign and trump occupy a path slightly above and ahead of the sphere of Venus. When that planet enters the world of the Tarot character it distorts his clear vision, bringing emotions into play that colours his understanding of the current situation. He can no longer judge what is reasonable. By nature this character relies on guidance from higher sources; they are small, subtle influences. The entry of Venus is like a hammer blow, although The Hermit is well equipped to deal with it. He has been this way before and he knows how to restore balance. Therefore the upset should be seen as a passing disturbance, not a warning of failure. It is the fire of Venus frustrating the earth of Virgo.

8 in 7

8= Mercury, 7= the star sign Libra and Tarot trump VIII, Adjustment. Mercury rules the element water, Libra is of air.

Weighing Memories

Moving home is a time for cleaning out dark corners. When we start afresh we do not like to leave behind our discarded remnants, nor do we like to carry unnecessary burdens. Only in times of established routine do we hoard the things we no longer treasure or need. We place them in dark corners where they will not disturb us.

Few have the strength of will to eject them on the day they cease to be of immediate value. They carry memories, and the memories are prized beyond the object itself. It is the memories we place in dark corners, where they will remain safe. Only when we must move on do we weigh those memories.

Weighing memories goes beyond emotion. We consider relevance, appropriateness, fitness; we judge their place in starting afresh. We clean out the dark corners without regret. Moving home is like all progress. Stepping forward is cleaner, simpler and less troublesome with a smaller load.

Summary

Moving home is an image of moving ahead, leaving the past behind and gaining new horizons. This will involve a restructuring of attitude. One must be prepared to let go with one hand and reach out with the other. It is difficult to see this in terms of sacrifice, for there is more to be gained than lost. What should be rejected is everything that no longer serves a purpose, as space will be required for more relevant acquisitions. These will not be restricted to material items, but will include new experiences and the memories they bestow. It is a sharpened approach that calls for the mind to be fully dedicated to the objective.

Conclusion

Mercury in Libra indicates accuracy of judgement and a sense of fair play. Libra's corresponding Tarot card, trump VIII, Adjustment, means treaties, partnerships, marriage, vindication of truth. On the Tree of Life the sign and trump occupy a path very close to the sphere of Mercury; in fact they form part of the triangle of Mercury, Mars and Sun. There is much about the trump that favours the Mercurial tendency to be emotionless and factual. The ability to make good decisions based on cold hard logic is a formidable trait of the Tarot character. The entrance of Mercury into her world accentuates this skill. It is the water of Mercury informing and refining the air of Libra.

9 in 8

9= Luna, 8= the star sign Scorpio and Tarot trump XIII, Death. Luna rules the element air, Scorpio is of water.

Making Entry

The crop is ready for harvest, but the harvester cannot approach his field. The way to the field is barred by many people going about their business. Most mean him no harm and spare him no attention; some take pleasure in deliberate obstruction. All humanity is there, on the way to the field.

The harvester must gather his crop. It is the season, the day and hour for gathering. He is one against many, but the many have no understanding of seasons, days and hours. They see only a harvester, one man among the crowd.

The harvester must be merciless. He must make entry to his field. To raise his scythe would be an error, invoking retribution. He must use his vision, his insight, to work his way through. If he acts with propriety he will gather the harvest.

Summary

The harvest is a symbol for the intended purpose, while the harvester is the person attempting to reach that end. But the way ahead is barred by ordinary people, or the minor hurdles they present, obstructing the harvester's needs and threatening the important harvest. A few try to obstruct him, but they have no honest grounds for doing so. There is limited time; it is the day and hour for gathering. With the goal so close and time so pressing, the harvester should spare no effort in making a way through the milling crowd. Aggressive tactics should be avoided at all costs; they will backfire. The crowd is not enough to put up an impassable barrier, but it does depend entirely on the faith and tenacity of the harvester.

Conclusion

Moon in Scorpio indicates ruthlessness and a lack of tact. Scorpio's corresponding Tarot card, trump XIII, Death, means change, a transformation of circumstances, starting afresh, destruction. (Please note that it does *not* portray or suggest physical death.) On the Tree of Life the sign and trump occupy a path slightly above the sphere of Moon. That planet's appearance in the world of the trump is a backward step, but it comes with an advantage. While it represents an aspect of the past, it is so closely related to the trump that the backward step obligingly points its own way forward. Vision and insight, or simply making the most of all possible advantages, will secure the way ahead. The harvester is not to be dismissed so easily; the milling crowd should worry for themselves. The harvest is there to be gathered. It is the air of Luna energizing the water of scythe-wielding Scorpio.

3 in 9

3= Saturn, 9= the star sign Sagittarius and Tarot trump XIV, Art. Saturn rules the element water, Sagittarius is of fire.

Water and Rock

The tall rock rises from the sea, like a dark finger pointing to the sky. It is weather-worn and old, encrusted with limpet shells. The waves beat upon it; breaking into spume they fall back upon themselves. The water and the rock know nothing of each other, yet they exist together. Knowing nothing of each other, the rock wears smooth, the sea pounds and gives way. The limpet shells have a home.

Tall and strong, the rock is imposing. It stands like a sentinel. Wide and deep, the sea is the mother of all things. Like a mother, she embraces the rock but to leave her mark takes time. The limpet shells increase daily. They are small and insignificant, yet their mark is made when and where they cling.

Summary

The rock can be seen on two levels. On one it is faith, conviction and aspiration rising from the depths of being. On the other it is suggestive of a person, upright and resolute in their ways, ambitious in their purpose. They are outstanding and because they are visible from a distance, likely to be successful. Like a rock they are not easily influenced and indeed may even be aloof to the feelings of others. The limpet shells are minor accretions, the multitude of gathered experiences which leave their mark but remain on the outside, where they are not allowed to have any influence. The sea represents one or more persons who are close and caring, but who seem to fail to win back the help or affection they display. They must work hard and over time to leave an impression, or gain what they need. It is an oracle of good omen in that the rock is outstanding and secure; yet it also paints a picture of people existing together but in different worlds, which is something unlikely to change any time soon.

Conclusion

Saturn in Sagittarius indicates high intellectual capacity and the ability to turn ideas into workable projects. The star sign's corresponding Tarot card, trump XIV, Art, means the combination of forces, the way of escape, harmonious partnerships, success. On the Tree of Life the sign and trump occupy an important path on the middle pillar, between the spheres of Moon and Sun. Saturn is a long way ahead, and its impact on the Tarot character will be one of stabilizing a given situation by the application of firm control. In the western mystery tradition the sphere of Saturn is the Great Sea, the silent yet productive Mother, hence the oceanic backdrop to the oracle. It is the nature of Saturn to be persistent, and if the waters had a mind to they would eventually wear the rock away completely. It is the water of Saturn limiting the fire of Sagittarius.

4 in 10

4= Jupiter, 10= the star sign Capricorn
and Tarot trump XV, The Devil.
Jupiter rules the element water, Capricorn is of earth.

Denial

The mountain goat has grown fat through indulgence. He is in danger of stumbling.

The once nimble climber of heights, steady in mind and body, picked as he chose from left and right. Not caring for what he picked, his hunger grew. Consuming became his passion.

The mountain is an unforgiving place. To walk its paths one must be sure-footed. It is not the true nature of the mountain goat to pick without caring. The effect on him will not reflect his true desires.

Picking without caring is a denial of self, of what is needed and fitting.

Summary

The image of a mountain goat growing fat is a symbol for a lack of care in attending to honest, inner values. Deep and fundamental convictions are being passed over, possibly to make gains in the world. Picking from left and right, or taking whatever seems convenient for the moment, only serves to make matters worse at a personal level. By ignoring inner values dissatisfaction increases; there follows a cruel spiral of convenience creating more discontent. The unforgiving mountain, which is life, will not shed any tears for those who are not true to themselves. This is the denial of self mentioned in the last line. It takes a good deal of courage to face one's self and be true to it, while keeping in mind the feelings of those who are close. Yet if they are close they will have seen glimpses of that self already, and perhaps that is why they have remained close.

Conclusion

Jupiter in Capricorn indicates the desire to amass wealth and gain influence over others. The star sign's corresponding Tarot card, trump XV, The Devil, means ambition, obsession, secret plans and activities, unscrupulous methods. On the Tree of Life the sign and trump are below but directly in line with the sphere of Jupiter. It is almost as if the Tarot character has Jupiter in his sights, and the two are on familiar terms; but first he must master the sphere of Sun. When Jupiter enters without the prior balancing and integrating powers of Sun, the Tarot character is swept away by material considerations which overpower his essential needs. It is the water of Jupiter engulfing the earth of Capricorn.

5 in 11

5= Mars, 11= the star sign Aquarius and Tarot trump XVII, The Star. Mars rules the element fire, Aquarius is of air.

The Cart

Pushing a cart uphill needs constant effort. If the effort is reduced the cart will roll back. Gained ground is lost.

A star that flickers is unstable. Bright one moment and dull the next, it is nearing the end of its purpose. Like the cart that advances and rolls back, it can be clearly seen by all who choose to look.

A star is beyond our help or control. We can do nothing for a flickering star. But a humble cart is within our power to control. They take much in the making, and repay us by carrying burdens for our use. They have their part to play. We lend a hand and help to push the cart.

Summary

Effort one moment, relaxing or inattention the next. It is not the way to succeed with certainty. The most important issue of this oracle is actually the one thing it does not mention; the road upon which the cart is placed. That road is the way to the desired end, but we must assume that the way itself is not under critical scrutiny: what matters is the means used to get there. The oracle introduces the flickering star as a way of indicating two salient points; there is no hiding this particular failing, and some matters, unlike the star, are completely within our control. The cart, which is the means employed to reach the chosen objective, is not being handled correctly, as if the willpower to achieve that end is lacking. But the closing lines tell us the end can be reached, so we do not stand by. We lend a hand, and with something like a spring-clean of attitude the wheels get moving.

Conclusion

Mars in Aquarius indicates a tendency to be erratic and non-conformist. The latter explains the choice of a cart as an analogy for a non-conformist means of carrying matters through; a cart is no longer common in today's high-tech world. The star sign's corresponding Tarot card, trump XVII, The Star, means unexpected help, increased vigour, new outlook. On the Tree of Life the sign and trump occupy the path between Sun and Neptune. Mars entering the world of the trump is a sign that disruption and contest are due to surface, and not necessarily from external sources. Hence, the back-and-forth progress of the cart. It is the fire of Mars searing the air of Aquarius.

6 in 12

6= Sun, 12= the star sign Pisces and Tarot trump XVIII, The Moon. Sun rules the element air, Pisces is of water.

The Roadside

A traveller sits by the roadside, watching the flow of people passing by. He is uncertain of his direction, envious of those who walk with purpose.

Quietly he sits, absorbed in his world of thoughts. He is hungry and thirsty, envious of those with their places to eat.

It is time for him to move on. He calls out for help to stand, for his legs are weak. The people move on without turning their heads.

Plunging deeper into gloom, the traveller stands abruptly and without thinking. He joins the flow of people. Without thinking he engages in cheerful conversation. Soon he is dining with new friends.

Sitting by the roadside is weak and unhelpful. When encountering a disagreeable sight people will move on without turning their heads.

Summary

Introspective, uncertain and easily confused, this traveller cannot stand on his own feet. He looks for help from others, when there is no real need to do so. He is perfectly able to take care of himself, yet he lives in a world of his own. If this is applied to a person the implications are clear enough. There is a need to gain more confidence, have a firmer belief in personal merit. That merit is there; it simply needs bringing to the surface. However, if this is applied to a situation it is a sign of an inherent weakness which needs to be addressed. There is an element lacking that needs building up if the situation is not to degenerate and spoil a potentially constructive outcome.

Conclusion

Sun in Pisces indicates the tendency to be impressionable and a little weak-willed. The star sign's corresponding Tarot card, trump XVIII, The Moon, means the brink, deception, a crisis of faith. It is perhaps the most dismal card of the pack. The entry of Sun into the world of this trump is beneficial in that it brings light where none existed previously. The worst tendencies are dramatically reduced, allowing a restoration of optimism. On the Tree of Life, Sun is higher aspected than the path of the sign and trump, which signals progress through difficult conditions. That progress will not come automatically; it must be given every help. It is the air of Sun attempting to breathe life into the dark waters of Pisces.

7 in 1

7= Venus, 1= the star sign Aries and Tarot trump IV, The Emperor. Venus rules the element fire, Aries is of fire.

Bounds of Reason

If he does not exercise caution, the emperor will act rashly.

Enthroned, he is in a position of power and authority. He has resources for achieving many ambitions. One is ahead of him now, ahead and within reach. It is his to take. In the taking there is danger of his fall.

When he takes what he wants he must be strong. To lose his values and judgement at the moment of his victory would see his realm fall into peril. What he takes has no disadvantage. The fault is with the emperor.

Impetuous and rash, he will celebrate beyond the bounds of reason. His authority will be diminished. What he takes, will end by overtaking him.

When approaching a ram, one should beware its horns.

Summary

The 'resources for achieving many ambitions' should be seen as personal abilities, rather than material aids. This is a case of ability winning the day, a time when matters fall into place. Yet in the winning there seems to be a danger, which has little or nothing to do with the objective in terms of hidden faults. It is more like biting off more than one can chew, or taking on something which, through its magnitude, ends in overpowering. The emperor, who may be one person or a collective, must keep a tight grip on matters if the success of achievement is not to end in disappointment. 'Approaching a ram' is a reference to Aries, which means ram, and signifies the emperor as he nears his chosen objective.

Conclusion

Venus in Aries indicates impulsiveness and the tendency to be extroverted. The star sign's corresponding Tarot card, trump IV, The Emperor, means vigour, conquest, ambition, rashness. On the Tree of Life the sign and trump occupy the path between Moon and Venus. The entry of Venus into the world of the trump suggests an ambition accomplished. The difficulty for the emperor is that he must then take on all the energies of Venus, which will have on him the effect of seeing everything in a rosy glow. The trump is not a stable card; it is in too early a stage of evolution to have gained strength and stability. He will find himself swimming in emotions instead of keeping a sharp lookout, as is appropriate for one in command. It is the fire of Venus and the fire of Aries combining in a blaze.

8 in 2

8= Mercury, 2= the star sign Taurus and Tarot trump V, The Hierophant. Mercury rules the element water, Taurus is of earth.

Management

The tall and strong tower was built many years past. The foundations were firm and they have stood the test of time.

Now the tower is put to a new use. There is pleasure in rearranging the interior. There is a sense of efficiency, a feeling of protection. What must be done is done with cheerful management.

People come and go in the busy tower; they see and approve the changes. Steadily it becomes a busy place; the sense of efficiency and protection increases.

In a final gesture the window shutters are thrown back. Light floods in. From inside the tower, the view outside brings great pleasure.

Summary

The tower is a place or condition of security. It is not new, having been established for some time. In this sense the tower can refer to an environment, or to a reliable person with a history of making sound decisions. The upsurge of activity signals that a new situation is about to dawn, in which efficiency and protection predominate. As this is done with 'cheerful management', it can be seen as changes willingly and happily accepted. The people coming and going are new lines of communication, which are part and parcel of the changes. Everything works well together, for the changes meet with approval. The light flooding in and the pleasing view are metaphors for visible improvements creating a better outlook.

Conclusion

Mercury in Taurus indicates the intelligent control of personal interests. The star sign's corresponding Tarot card, trump V, The Hierophant, means stubborn strength, toil, wise counsel, the comfort of religion. On the Tree of Life the sign and trump occupy the path between Jupiter and Neptune. This is a high and important location, and the entry of lower aspected Mercury into the world of the trump indicates a backward step. In a spiritual sense this is true, for the trump has little in common with Mercury. But the planet represents the messenger of the gods, and although sometimes given to trickery Mercury is above all a communicator of the divine. The trump's character, The Hierophant, is a teacher, a revealer of secrets. (He is actually the tower of strength in the oracle.) There is therefore a similarity of external function between the planet and trump, which will have different consequences in the material world to those in the spiritual. In the material world this will manifest as inventiveness and a good business sense, although for the oracle the overall theme and the marrying of forces is more important than business specifics. It is the water of Mercury embracing the earth of Taurus.

9 in 3

9= Luna, 3= the star sign Gemini and Tarot trump VI, The Lovers. Luna rules the element air, Gemini is of air.

Beginning and Preparing

The two lovers have many dreams, many ambitions. To make them real the lovers begin to prepare. They count their ambitions and reach a large number. Setting to work at once they hurry from here to there, beginning and preparing. This takes them through the first day.

On the next day they count their dreams. Reaching a large number they set to work at once. They hurry from here to there, beginning and preparing.

At the end of that day they have no strength. Sitting at rest they discuss their dreams and recount their ambitions. Contented and exhausted, they sleep.

The following day they awaken in sorrow. They cannot remember where they began their labours, or where their labours ended. The numbers were too large, the distance covered was too wide. Shadows follow the two lovers, as they part their separate ways in search of their dreams and ambitions.

Summary

Too many options spread too wide, too many irons in the fire at one time, or too many undertakings started but not seen through; the oracle can mean any or all of these things in one sweep. Hurried activity in excessive directions will detract from any hope of success. Equally the same principle applies where there are not many but one endeavour; insufficient attention is given to the primary aim. When effort is spread out so thinly, the only probable result is failure. The two lovers may be two people, or one person and their chosen objective. In either case an urgent review of method is the next important step.

Conclusion

Luna in Gemini indicates a vivid imagination and a tendency to daydream. Gemini's corresponding Tarot card, trump VI, The Lovers, means inspiration, childishness, swift adaptability. On the Tree of Life the sign and trump occupy the path between Sun and Saturn. They are considerably ahead of the sphere of Moon; when that planet (i.e. Luna) enters the world of the trump it is a negative sign. All progress is disturbed by unwelcome destabilizing forces. Luna introduces a tidal pull that sets unsettling waves in motion. It is the air of Luna and the air of Gemini combining to displace and erode, rather than create.

3 in 4

3= Saturn, 4= the star sign Cancer and Tarot trump VII, The Chariot. Saturn rules the element water, Cancer is of water.

Unassailable

The battleground is to the rear; the battle is won. The charioteer leaves unscathed.

He does not return to his familiar land, but follows instead a new and straight road. His chariot and steeds have a hill to climb; it is steep and leads to the House of Influence. There he will be made welcome. On his arrival he can set his steeds free, and put aside his chariot. He can remove his weapons and armour without regret.

The charioteer has grown neither old nor infirm; he has gathered more strength and become unassailable. He can lay down the things that served him well. The House of Influence is where he belongs.

Summary

The days of contest and struggle are over and in the past. The charioteer moves on without suffering defeat. Ahead is a new direction, and while it will incur its own demands they will be manageable. The chariot, steeds, armour and weapons are the ways and means used to bring him to this point; they are very much a part of what he is. Now however, he need rely only on himself. The root of this oracle is in the person; it is the individual that counts above all else. There is a recognition of special merit and achievement, which serves to raise this charioteer to a new and rewarding level.

Conclusion

Saturn in Cancer indicates a strong desire for emotional and material security. Cancer's corresponding Tarot card, trump VII, The Chariot, means triumph, hope, faithfulness, obedience. On the Tree of Life the sign and trump occupy a high and significant path between the spheres of Mars and Saturn. The entry of Saturn into the world of the trump shows that Mars with its war-like nature is to the rear, or in the past, while the ultimate objective of Saturn has been (or is due to be) reached. The House of Influence is the name of the path on the Tree which leads to Saturn, while the sphere of Saturn itself is known in the Sepher Yetzirah (the book mentioned in chapter 2) as the Sanctifying Intelligence. The latter represents a stage of spiritual progress without parallel in the material world, and only the path of entry can really be described. In the world of daily affairs it signifies a high point of deserved success. It is the water of Saturn merging as one with the water of Cancer.

4 in 5

4= Jupiter, 5= the star sign Leo and Tarot trump XI, Lust.
Jupiter rules the element water, Leo is of fire.

Unbreakable

The naked woman dismounts from the great wild lion. She has ridden the beast over a long and difficult journey. The apparently weak and the manifestly strong were joined in a mutual quest; now they have reached their destination.

Beneath the surface the woman and the lion are equals, yet opposites. Like two weights upon scales their inner natures balance. Maintaining that balance and their union has brought them this far; now it is time to savour the rewards of joining together.

Although the woman dismounts she will never part from the lion; although the lion has no rider he will always bear her with him. Their union is unbreakable; they are one.

This destination they reach is a place of blessings, of all good things.

Summary

The Tarot characters can be seen as two people or one person and their desired ambition. A balanced approach has terminated at a desired end, yet it does not mark the end of a mutual accord, or the laying to one side of previously useful attributes. These still have their part to play, although from this point on they are likely to serve new purposes. This desired end, which due to the nature of the trump is a significant phase in life, marks an important accomplishment of united effort. It is a case of appropriate action taken at the appropriate time, and where hurdles have been encountered and overcome. Like minds have worked together; their labour has rewarded them with a stable and enduring finish.

Conclusion

Jupiter in Leo indicates a highly creative and confident approach to life. Leo's corresponding Tarot card, trump XI, Lust, means courage, strength, energy and action. On the Tree of Life the sign and trump occupy the path between the spheres of Mars and Jupiter. The appearance of Jupiter in the world of the trump demonstrates a destination reached, an ambition accomplished. Jupiter is strong, stable and bestows abundance, in the same way that Jupiter in the guise of the sea god Poseidon bestows abundance in the waters. The woman and lion Tarot characters are representative of what is ultimately a single creative force, hence the oracle's line; 'Their union is unbreakable; they are one'. It is the water of Jupiter and the fire of Leo meeting as equals and rising in majesty.

5 in 6

5= Mars, 6= the star sign Virgo and Tarot trump IX, The Hermit. Mars rules the element fire, Virgo is of earth.

The Storm

The hermit opens the door to his hermitage without looking outside. He does not see what is beyond his walls; he does not see the approaching storm.

Returning to his seat, the hermit resumes his meditations. He has opened the door, but he returns to his own world.

A storm strikes where it will. It shows no favour; it takes down the great and the small. What is strong can resist; what is weak will fall. What is open will allow entry; whether great, small, strong or weak, a storm will enter when the way is open.

Life is full of doorways, though many are not recognised as such. Those who understand this, yet act without prudence are like the hermit. He meditates while the storm seeks his door.

Summary

Wheels have been set in motion that will bring unfortunate consequences. A single act, possibly with every good intention, sometimes can be enough to create misunderstanding and lead to conflict. The hermit has opened such a door; the fact that he has returned to his own world is a sign that he is blissfully unaware of any approaching trouble. That at least is one interpretation; the other is that he may well have deliberately chosen not to see, and carried on regardless as though nothing was about to happen. This is not fiddling while Rome burns, for as yet there are no visible fires. But they will come, and in such a way that they will take no account of where and how they strike; 'whether great, small, strong or weak, a storm will enter'. It is clearly better to make peace, or settle trouble in the making, before matters reach that stage.

Conclusion

Mars in Virgo indicates misplaced ideals and friction with associates. Virgo's corresponding Tarot card, trump IX, The Hermit, means illumination from within, practical plans, isolation, discretion. On the Tree of Life the sign and trump occupy a path between the spheres of Sun and Jupiter, where their respective titles of Beauty and Mercy reflect qualities ideal for the hermit's meditations. Mars is a step to the side and brings no benefit. The essence of the trump is the potential of fertility; the crude business of Mars is to wreak havoc. It is the fire of Mars attempting to destroy the earth of Virgo.

6 in 7

6= Sun, 7= the star sign Libra and Tarot trump VIII, Adjustment. Sun rules the element air, Libra is of air.

The Confident Voice

The woman stands tall and straight. She has nothing to fear, nothing to hide. She is in a place of good friends.

Her past has known darkness and light, worry and happiness. Her strength has brought her this far, where she can stand tall and straight. Now her way ahead is clear; it calls to her with a confident voice. What remains in the past has its place in the past. The woman has a mind only for the way ahead, and she listens to the confident voice.

Friends gather where there is no conflict. A place of good friends is a house without disagreement. Partnerships are born here, and new bonds emerge. Full of light, a place of good friends is a stepping stone to a brighter light. Facing that light, all her shadows will remain harmlessly behind.

Summary

The woman is a direct reference to the Tarot character, a figure representing the continuous adjustment of life's diverse twists and turns in a move to gain a sense of order and harmony. Past efforts have brought her to a position where her efforts have paid dividends, for the 'place of good friends' signifies harmonious surroundings. There is no conflict. She has a pretty clear idea of the route ahead, hence the confident voice that she can hear, and it is a fortunate direction. Fortunate times will enhance existing relationships and bring new contacts; it is a good omen for both social and material gain. The stepping stone to a brighter light is a metaphor for better times ahead, where there will be little need to look back.

Conclusion

Sun in Libra indicates a need for company and a desire for harmony. Libra's corresponding Tarot card, trump VIII, Adjustment, means partnerships, marriage, vindication of truth. On the Tree of Life the sign and trump occupy the path between Sun and Mars. The appearance of Sun in the world of the trump shows the Tarot character is ideally placed for a new beginning, with all surrounding issues being well-placed to contribute to a successful future. There is one reservation in that the path leads to Mars, where there will be unavoidable discord and turbulence. This is a long way ahead, and by that time the Tarot character will have learned all she needs to know in order to deal with it. For the moment, it is the air of Sun joining the air of Libra in a breath of summer.

7 in 8

7= Venus, 8= the star sign Scorpio and Tarot trump XIII, Death. Venus rules the element fire, Scorpio is of water.

The Iron Grip

The harvester is inspired by exciting visions. He sees new ways to turn his field to advantage. Taking up his scythe, he approaches the crop with high expectations.

He sweeps his scythe to left and right, vigorous and confident. He cuts down brambles, weeds and wild grasses. There is no corn in this field, or other edible harvest. It has never been planted. But the harvester has his exciting visions.

It matters not how long or hard he labours. He will gain nothing of value. The field is what it is.

Exciting visions have the power to hold in an iron grip. They are fueled by hope and desire. Visions, hope and desire; the three have no substance, they cannot be held. Yet like phantoms they possess the living, and the living bid them welcome.

Summary

A new idea or objective seems to offer potential; there is something to be had from it, but a more critical look will reveal fundamental flaws. What appears worth going for is not as it seems; too much will be lost in the process. The living bid these phantoms welcome for hope and desire overrule any inclination to see matters as they are. The need is so great that failure cannot be contemplated, and in consequence risky undertakings are fully embraced. The message of the oracle is clear; this is a path fraught with danger.

Conclusion

Venus in Scorpio indicates a tendency towards self-indulgence and idealism. Scorpio's corresponding Tarot card, trump XIII, Death, means change, transformation, starting afresh. (Please note the trump does not mean or imply physical death.) On the Tree of Life the sign and trump occupy the path between Venus and Sun. The entry of Venus into the world of the trump shows that nothing is out of place, yet the oracle is negative. This is due to the Tarot character being swamped by the forces of Venus. Although a potent card in a mystical sense, in the material world much of that potency is watered down, as confirmed by its purely divinatory meanings. (All Tarot cards are double-edged swords in this respect.) The Tarot character has yet to acquire the inner strength necessary to master the forces of Venus when they alone dominate, the net result being an over-optimistic view to the point of an extreme type of faith, where nothing is questioned. It is the fire of Venus bringing a false rose glow to the water of Scorpio.

8 in 9

8= Mercury, 9= the star sign Sagittarius and Tarot trump XIV, Art. Mercury rules the element water, Sagittarius is of fire.

The Hinge

Into the magic cauldron go the ingredients of mystery; herbs and spices from far-away lands, bones and dust from the sellers of secrets. The woman stirs the brew; she knows her art. She has a gift for the creation of wonders.

Day and night she labours without rest, always stirring, always creating. At length it is complete.

Her apprentice watches, his eyes wide. He sees her take a small drop from the cauldron, and apply it to the hinge of her door. She tries the door. The hinge no longer squeaks.

The woman sits down in complete satisfaction.

Her apprentice leaves for home, vowing never to return.

Summary

A massive expenditure of effort for little return; a misapplication of skills to a trivial purpose; a failure to see in advance an easier way to achieve the same end. The oracle means all of these things. There is a mind of good intellect in control of the proceedings, yet there is a failure to identify the shortest and best way through surrounding issues. There is no fault with the intention; it is the contorted means to get there that receives all the criticism. It may well be that the stirring has yet to start. If this is the case, leave everything as it is and look at the issue afresh. It will save time and effort.

Conclusion

Mercury in Sagittarius indicates a traditional outlook, a preference for established routines. The star sign's corresponding Tarot card, trump XIV, Art, means action based on calculation, joining forces, the way of escape. On the Tree of Life the sign and trump occupy the path between Moon and Sun on the important middle pillar. The entry of Mercury into the world of the Tarot character indicates a sideways step, a distraction from the straight and narrow. It allows the trickster in Mercury to run riot and play every trick in his book. That is why there is no criticism of the intended objective, only the way of going about it. It is the water of Mercury confounding the fire of Sagittarius.

9 in 10

9= Luna, 10= the star sign Capricorn and Tarot trump XV, The Devil. Luna rules the element air, Capricorn is of earth.

Integrity

The dark stranger enters his chosen place, where there are many people. The people fall silent; they watch the dark stranger as he takes his seat in a prominent position.

Some whisper that he has authority; others say that he is one to beware.

If he acts now with true friendship and generosity, the people will take to him and call him friend. Their doubts will be removed. Should he act with cunning and words with two meanings, some people will call him friend while others will dismiss him. There will be disagreement among the people.

When gathering support, integrity is a key virtue. When assessing a stranger, his words are the signposts of his integrity. If they ring false or contain double meanings, the people must ask why he has chosen their company.

Summary

This oracle can apply on two levels. It can refer to the approach of someone aiming for their chosen goal, or it can relate to the person or persons closely linked to that goal. The bottom line is duplicity, the intention to convey an impression that is not entirely accurate. Something is being kept back, or left unsaid. This may amount to no more than a reluctance to admit to embarrassing skeletons in the cupboard, rather than any intentional aim to score an undeserved advantage. The circumstances and their gravity must be assessed for themselves. But the indications are that not everything is being revealed, and there is always the chance that truth will out. The mere fact that it has been raised by the oracle suggests that it will.

Conclusion

Luna in Capricorn indicates a tendency to use people for self-advancement. Capricorn's corresponding Tarot card, trump XV, The Devil, means ambition, blind impulse, secret plans, unscrupulous methods. On the Tree of Life the sign and trump occupy the path between Mercury and Sun. The entrance of Moon in the world of the Tarot character is a slightly backward step; not enough to cause total disruption, but sufficient to allow the forces of deception to manifest and take over. It is the air of Moon smothering the earth of Capricorn with dust.

3 in 11

3= Saturn, 11= the star sign Aquarius and Tarot trump XVII, The Star. Saturn rules the element water, Aquarius is of air.

The Friendly Voice

Adrift at sea, the small boat is tossed by waves. The people on board are in need of help; they have lost count of their days on the ocean.

The people talk among themselves, bravely they keep their spirits high.

The ocean is vast, with no end in sight. Nowhere can they see land. All is emptiness, all is hostile. The small boat is an island of memories and hope. Another night falls and the people sleep, while the stars look down with their undiminished light.

With the coming of dawn the people are stirred by a friendly voice calling. Like a mountain on the sea a large ship is close by. From out of the waves, from out of all hopelessness, help has arrived.

Summary

As if lost at sea, there is the impression that there is no place of refuge, no solid base to rely on. There is no certainty or sense of direction, only feelings of helplessness in a hostile world. Those who are close offer what encouragement they can, but their words can do little to offset the anxiety. The only reliable constant is the starlight, which remains undiminished. This image is introduced by the oracle as a reminder that there is always hope, sometimes from directions we do not fully understand, or in ways which are completely unexpected. That is the case here, when there is a break in the current of gloom.

The situation is restored in a manner that promises firm control, avoiding a return to this sea of desolation.

Conclusion

Saturn in Aquarius indicates a tendency to hold fixed and limiting ideas. The star sign's corresponding Tarot card, trump XVII, The Star, means clearness of vision, increased vigour, expansion of horizons. On the Tree of Life the sign and trump occupy a high and important path between Sun and Neptune. The entry of Saturn into the world of the trump is a step to one side, and we must question why this would need to take place. The Tarot character has no need of Saturn's ability to impose control unless one other divinatory meaning of the card is taken into account – unexpected help. This could only occur if the character has become lost on her upward journey. This journey takes her through a testing and dangerous region of the Tree, and she has such close links with Saturn that the planet would be a natural guide in times of difficulty. In short, Saturn would not have made its entry on the stage unless a need existed. It is an oracle of optimism, showing a way ahead after a period of seeming hopelessness. The waters of Saturn uplift the air of Aquarius.

4 in 12

4= Jupiter, 12= the star sign Pisces and Tarot trump XVIII, The Moon. Jupiter rules the element water, Pisces is of water.

The Net

In his small boat upon the lake, the fisherman hauls his catch. It is night, with a full moon, the lake's best time for a full and profitable net. He unloads the net into the small boat, spilling out hundreds of fine fish. Their bodies are silver coins in the making.

He surveys the silver, watching it writhe. This is his life, his nightly work, and the fish are his food and income. Yet tonight and for the first time he sees them as living things. He feels their panic. He considers that it has always been thus, and will continue forever. People eat the fish, the fish eat each other. It is the way of life; it will never change. Yet in this moment he has changed. He understands the needs of all creatures. He understands the dreadful power of his net.

Summary

The fish represent all life, all creatures – including and more to the point, people. This oracle is not concerned with winning or losing, success or failure, whatever the question might have been. It exposes a more fundamental issue; that of an attitude to others, and this must be seen in relation to the question. The oracle does not suggest that the fisherman is callous or selfish – far from it. He is an ordinary person going about his honest business. But a change takes place. There is a new and deeper understanding of life as seen through the eyes of others, and how this reflects on the role he plays. His net is the means he uses to connect and communicate with those around him, or who are important to him. It has a dreadful power if used without care. Correctly employed, it will enhance the way he is perceived and regarded.

Conclusion

Jupiter in Pisces indicates a tendency to extravagance, and sometimes a lack of consistency. There may also be philosophical leanings. The star sign's corresponding Tarot card, trump XVIII, The Moon, means illusion, deception, a crisis of faith, the brink. On the Tree of Life the sign and trump occupy the path between Earth and Venus. The entry of Jupiter into the world of the trump shows a giant leap ahead, for the trump is a base and undeveloped affair while Jupiter is a mighty and beneficial force. The nature of the trump forbids any kind of unexpected wealth or abundance, which would sometimes be the case with Jupiter's influence, but there will be benefits of a different order. The dismal and unbalanced tone of The Moon trump is refined and steadied, and in consequence reflects the world in a better, more balanced light. It is the water of Jupiter clarifying the water of Pisces.

5 in 1

5= Mars, 1= the star sign Aries and Tarot trump IV, The Emperor. Mars rules the element fire, Aries is of fire.

Expertise

The emperor has taken on his armour. His heart is full of fury and his sword is in his hand. He is eager for the battle, ready to claim his victory.

His advisors gather round, offering words of counsel. They remind him of the need for caution. Those who advance in fury look only ahead, or to their left and right; they do not sense the coward behind them. The emperor must temper his enthusiasm with a general's skills. He must contain his passion.

More battles are won by expertise than by force of numbers. The best battles are never fought. They remain as theories, while old men sit and talk in halls of power. Two combatants, one bottle of finest wine. The better the vine, the better the fruit.

Summary

There is not so much a battle ahead; this is simply a caution that a current situation could easily lead to avoidable friction. The emperor is not given to pulling his punches at the best of times, and any hint of a disagreement could escalate unnecessarily. It is a time for controlling any sense of annoyance or frustration. There are other roads to victory. The mention of wine is not to be taken literally; it is a reference to the Sufi saints and poets, who used wine as a metaphor in their writings. The vine is the school of teaching, the fruit is the product of that school, and the wine is the resultant transmission of knowledge. Put another way, forethought and words will succeed in the present case far better than any display of resentment. This destabilizing circumstance occurs as if by chance, rather than any deliberate attempt to provoke. It is better to seek another route if at all possible.

Conclusion

Mars in Aries indicates the tendency to act without consideration for other people. The star sign's corresponding Tarot card, trump IV, The Emperor, means rule, conquest, energy, quarrelsomeness. On the Tree of Life the sign and trump occupy the path between Moon and Venus, with Mars waiting two steps ahead. This distance represents too much progress for the emperor to accommodate. He is not yet a stable character, being the first appearance of the fire element, reflecting the swift and creative way that Aries opens up the year. When the energies of Mars enter his world, it is fire meeting fire with disastrous consequences. As no one would willingly put themselves in this position, it is likely to seem more by chance than design. The fires of Mars combine with those of Aries to create a volcano.

6 in 2

6= Sun, 2= the star sign Taurus and Tarot trump V, The Hierophant. Sun rules the element air, Taurus is of earth.

The Important Rose

On this day, the teacher is taking no classes. He leads the way in many areas, spreading his skills to benefit those in his charge. He is solid, dependable. To uphold his position he works hard to raise the value of his knowledge, and his capacity to care. Already he knows much, yet he steps back now to remember.

He considers his early beginnings, and the vows he once made. Aware of his responsibilities, he fears losing his original aims. With the passage of time, and with information gathered like rose petals, it is easy to wander from a once simple course. Complexity of learning builds its own roads. They go where they will, guided only by a desirable perfume.

It is well for the teacher to remember. It is well for him to recall his most important rose.

Summary

The teacher represents someone held in regard and to whom other people turn for support. This support may be emotional, financial or both. Circumstances dictate the need to step back for a personal review, to assess the direction of life at this time and consider whether it is in line with a preferred course. This will be at the root of all decisions concerning choices soon to be made which impact on the future. The review is a major part of making the right choices. To proceed purely for the sake of an easy option would not result in long-term satisfaction.

The oracle is really saying decide what you need at a personal level before going any further.

Conclusion

Sun in Taurus indicates a desire for emotional and material security. The star sign's corresponding Tarot card, trump V, The Hierophant, means wise counsel, stubborn strength, teaching, goodness of heart. On the Tree of Life the sign and trump occupy a high path between Jupiter and Neptune. The entry of Sun into the world of the Tarot character indicates a slight step back, although for The Hierophant this is not a complete disadvantage. Sun brings tranquility; the name of its sphere on the Tree is Beauty, which sums up its balancing and harmonious forces. These are basic requirements for a teacher with goodness of heart, and go a long way to fulfilling the trump's additional meaning of peace. It is the air of Sun informing the earth of Taurus.

7 in 3

7= Venus, 3= the star sign Gemini and Tarot trump VI, The Lovers. Venus rules the element fire, Gemini is of air.

Two Trees

Two trees stand side by side. They have been this way since their beginning. From saplings they have matured into mighty oaks; their branches and their roots entwine. No axe will ever fall upon this precious sight. The forest may be cleared; these two will remain.

Water and soil are their only needs. From water they build new boughs and leaves; from a thing as gentle as rain they make bodies as hard as stone. No need of speech, no need of movement, they grow and endure through the ages.

We may ask of their purpose. We may question why such miracles need exist. The trees know only growth and endurance. They know nothing of wealth, wisdom, war.

The trees will stand long after those who question can no longer see them.

Summary

The two trees may be two people, or one person and their objective. Here there is a similarity of purpose, a virtual joining of souls. The ties are so strong as to be outstanding; nothing will easily part them. Capable and resourceful, something of little regard can be transformed into a useful commodity. There is a likeness of mind that sees each acting with the same purpose, without the need for consultation. They do what they do for themselves, and without reference to others. Their actions bring harm to no one; it is not in their nature to cause harm.

Their contentment is in sharing; it is an arrangement that will stand the long test of time.

Conclusion

Venus in Gemini indicates a tendency to be charming and sociable. Gemini's corresponding Tarot card, trump VI, The Lovers, means intuition, intelligence, openness to inspiration. On the Tree of Life the sign and trump occupy a high path between Sun and Saturn. The entry of lower aspected Venus indicates a reaffirming of objectives, rather than a negative backward step. It is a pause in which the figure of Cupid (or Eros), depicted in the trump, has the opportunity to make his presence felt once more. The Lovers in the trump are represented by the two trees, for the underlying meaning of the card is the act of creation in a universal sense. This act is far greater than humble mankind, and the image of two oaks conveys more readily the sense of power and timelessness. It is the fire of Venus inspiring the air of Gemini.

8 in 4

8= Mercury, 4= the star sign Cancer and Tarot trump VII, The Chariot. Mercury rules the element water, Cancer is of water.

Contingency

Holding the reins tightly, the charioteer steers his chariot through uncharted lands. His steeds are fresh and fleet; their hooves pound the soil.

The path ahead is not clear, yet the charioteer has a will to press on. The uncharted lands lead to a place of legendary repute. It is the charioteer's temperament to be ruthless and determined; nothing will bar his way. He is prepared for every contingency.

He travels east and west, establishing camps which may prove useful. He seeks out rivers in one valley, wild game in another, for they too may prove useful. He assesses forests for yielding lances and spears; he looks for a village wherein a blacksmith may live, should the wheels of his chariot need repair. Hour by hour, he covers more contingencies.

He rests the first night, content that his journey goes well.

Summary

His journey is going nowhere. The charioteer, for all his skill and "diehard" approach to life, has not refined his efforts to one purpose. Acting out of character, he has given his plan a great deal of thought and then applied his sharp intelligence to unhelpful peripheral details. It would be more like him to crack the whip and get the horses up to speed in a straight line. He is ruthless and determined. The only asset he needs is himself. Those about to meet him for the first time will not fail to recognise his personal merits. Those who already know him are fully familiar with those merits. They do not need to see him dotting i's and crossing t's. He is simply taking on too much. He will succeed in the end, for that is his will, and there really is no need for such doubt or caution.

Conclusion

Mercury in Cancer indicates a good memory and a keen imagination. Cancer's corresponding Tarot card, trump VII, The Chariot, means triumph, hope, faithfulness, success through initiative. On the Tree of Life the sign and trump occupy a high and important path between the spheres of Mars and Saturn. The entry of Mercury is a step back, effectively introducing trains of thought that have no business in the world of the Tarot character. He subsides from a bull in a china shop to being a theorist. He is ruthless for his spiritual quest is of prime importance, and he will use any means at his disposal to succeed. As a Tarot character, however, those means consist of himself and nothing else. He needs nothing else. Here we see the water of Mercury and the water of Cancer producing needless rivulets.

9 in 5

9= Luna, 5= the star sign Leo and Tarot trump XI, Lust.
Luna rules the element air, Leo is of fire.

The Dwarf and the Giant

A dwarf and a giant are not well-matched in size. When they are to travel together, they must reach an agreement. Each must recognise the other's needs, and not deny them. Then the dwarf and the giant together may go where they will.

Tall or short, weak or strong; these measures have nothing in common with desire. Desire has no dimensions. The desire of the giant may be surpassed by that of the dwarf. No one can make a purse to contain desire.

When the dwarf claims rights not in keeping with reality, the giant has only to stride away. The dwarf will not keep up, no matter what he spends from his purse.

Footsteps can be measured; wishes and desires cannot.

Summary

Whether the querent is seen as the dwarf or giant must depend on the circumstances surrounding the question. But the inescapable fact is that there is a conflict of interests. What one desires, the other does not. The footsteps of the giant should be seen as achievements; they are the measurable advances made through personal efforts. By itself a desire or wish, on the other hand, has no quantifiable background, no way of proving itself. Unless there is a monument of sorts to a desire or wish being worked into measurable results, they will remain intangible and possibly fail to gain support. Hard evidence is best, especially when hoping to make an impression.

Conclusion

Luna in Leo indicates a dramatic and self-centered personality. Leo's corresponding Tarot card, trump XI, Lust, means courage, strength, energy and action. On the Tree of Life the sign and trump occupy the path between the spheres of Mars and Jupiter. These are dramatically conflicting spheres, and the trump shows how to keep them in balance. The entry of Luna into the world of the trump is unfortunate. Although there are definite links between Luna and the trump these do not bode well in the material world. Luna seeks to influence the woman character to the detriment of the male lion. She begins to experience ideas and visions that have more in keeping with dreams than practicalities. The result is an imbalance in their union. It is the air of Luna raising the fire of Leo to furnace heat.

3 in 6

3= Saturn, 6= the star sign Virgo and Tarot trump IX, The Hermit. Saturn rules the element water, Virgo is of earth.

The Owl

On a small island in a great ocean, a figure sits in meditation. He hears the waves upon the shore. It is night.

A passing owl asks him how he can shut himself away, yet be fit to live in his own world. The owl has no understanding of spirituality, or self, or illumination. It knows only the way of owls.

The man answers that he has no wings; he cannot fly and must therefore walk. By shutting himself away, he can ponder the art of walking correctly in his world.

The owl then asks why he chooses an island in a great ocean. The man answers that once there was a man who learned to walk so well, he could walk upon water.

The owl considers this. He asks what happened to a man so clever.

"He became a dove," said the man. The wise owl took off, hunting for mice.

Summary

Some things make sense, some apparently do not. What the meditating figure has just realised is that some objectives involve a major shift in mind-set. Not only that, it takes a special kind of person to reach the highest levels of achievement. There is something vaguely "going round in circles" about this unusual oracle: if learning to walk (or learning the way to success) is his ambition, why end as a metaphoric bird –

something completely different. The owl saw this at once, but being wise said nothing. The meditating figure is at a crossroads. He certainly has the acumen to succeed, but perhaps a new understanding has revealed that his present course should be adjusted. Perhaps the goal itself is now seen as questionable, or a prior attitude towards it has taken on a different light. He alone can judge, for the influence upon him is one of extreme self-judgement. What is telling, however, is that this need for extreme self-judgement has arisen.

Conclusion

Saturn in Virgo indicates a tendency to be severe and practical. Virgo's corresponding Tarot card, trump IX, The Hermit, means isolation, withdrawal, illumination from within, practical plans. On the Tree of Life the sign and trump occupy the path between the spheres of Sun and Jupiter. Saturn is a good way ahead, and will have a major impact on the lower aspected Tarot character. Saturn's forces of strict regulation and control will swing into play; yet so too will its ability to evoke a profound understanding of life. The combination of control and understanding will materialise as the need to be in charge of circumstances and comprehend where one is going; hence the strict self-judgement. It is the water of Saturn bearing down on the soil of Virgo.

4 in 7

4= Jupiter, 7= the star sign Libra and Tarot trump VIII, Adjustment. Jupiter rules the element water, Libra is of air.

Circle and Square

The scales of nature will always balance. When the scales are out of true, the weights are adjusted. The left hand gives to the right hand; the right hand gives to the left. There is no true growth, only a dividing and sharing.

Constant dividing and sharing is like a circle; it allows movement, but remains unchanged. It stays a circle. The way of life does not alter.

To make a square from the circle one must adopt new methods. A bold approach will break through barriers. When barriers are removed the way of life is free to proceed where it wills, construct new shapes as it wills. Barriers are restrictions; they are the enemy of all freedom. Test the circle; discover the breach.

Summary

Dividing and sharing is a routine, the play of life that goes on without need of a script, for the end is predictable. When change is sought new methods are in order. Earning, paying out, gaining, losing; all these are the familiar elements of life, the actors on our personal stage. To make fundamental changes one must be bold. However, there is a difference between boldness and folly. The oracle advises to test the circle, that is, act with due attention to the rules. Throwing caution to the winds is not advisable, unless one has an inexhaustible supply of resources to cover any losses. The oracle's bottom line shows high optimism and is an omen of good fortune. The advice would not be offered if it were not possible to achieve.

Conclusion

Jupiter in Libra indicates someone with a cooperative spirit, and a strong sense of fairness. Libra's corresponding Tarot card, trump VIII, Adjustment, means partnerships, marriage, negotiations, the vindication of truth. On the Tree of Life the sign and trump occupy the path between the spheres of Sun and Mars, where a good deal of adjustment is required to mediate between the two very different forces. Jupiter is a step ahead, and its entrance into the world of the Tarot character brings far-reaching changes. The enormous stabilizing qualities of Jupiter serve to elevate the character, injecting new strength and virility. This makes possible the change of scene from circle to square, or from one long-established set of circumstances to something entirely new. It is the water of Jupiter delivering the chance of abundance to Virgo.

5 in 8

5= Mars, 8= the star sign Scorpio and Tarot trump XIII, Death. Mars rules the element fire, Scorpio is of water.

Talent and Aptitude

When people see the harvester scything down his crop with vigour and enthusiasm, they prepare for a generous harvest.

One harvester, one scythe; so little against the big field. As he begins to claim the harvest, the people acknowledge his skills. They praise his talent and aptitude. They wonder at his vigour and enthusiasm.

The harvester sees only the field, the extent of his labour. He reaps for it is his will to reap. He knows others will benefit, but his pleasure is in sowing well, reaping well. His pleasure is in his conduct.

When his work is done the grain stores will be filled.

Summary

Sound beginnings culminate in a plentiful harvest. This is down to the efforts and dedication of one person. They are not out to impress, and financial reward is not their main motive; they follow their inner driving force. While they may be satisfied to see others gaining as a result, their greatest satisfaction is in their personal achievement. They will make difficult choices without flinching, if those choices will serve their own ends. In this respect they are not selfish; they are out to do their very best, and others must be prepared to accept this fact. In the end, everyone shares the benefits.

Conclusion

Mars in Scorpio indicates a person with ruthless survival instincts. Scorpio's corresponding Tarot card, trump XIII, Death, means sudden change, transformation, starting afresh. (Please note it does not mean or suggest physical death.) On the Tree of Life the sign and trump occupy the path between the spheres of Venus and Sun. Mars is not only a step ahead, it is also a direct extension of the existing path. The Tarot character is well-equipped to confront the war-like forces of Mars; he is quite used to wielding a sharp and terrible weapon. His experience transmutes these divisive forces into their subtlest forms; from turbulence and destruction he extracts vigour and enthusiasm. Had the symbolism of Scorpio not included the lofty eagle, as the exaltation of the highest above solid matter, then the scythe could well have become a murderous threat. As it is, the harvester heads towards a deserved achievement. It is the fire of Mars enthusing the water of Scorpio.

6 in 9

6= Sun, 9= the star sign Sagittarius and Tarot trump XIV, Art. Sun rules the element air, Sagittarius is of fire.

Eagle and Lion

With her cauldron lit, the woman attempts to create perfection. She takes ingredients without life, and casts them into the mix.

Watching her is a white eagle and a red lion. They are at her side; together they oversee her every move.

She stirs the embers until the flames meet with her approval; she stirs the mix until vapours arise. The eagle and the lion grow hopeful. They see the arrival of success.

All these things seem matters of fancy, and not of this world. The woman, the cauldron, the lion and the eagle cannot be found in the world we know. Yet the woman creates perfection; the red lion has become white, and the white eagle becomes red. Within the cauldron is new life. Where there is great success, those who can see are familiar with matters of fancy, matters not of this world. The woman, the cauldron, the lion, the eagle and new life are visible everywhere.

Summary

Undoubtedly the most mystical of all the oracles, this is a comment on the age-old art of alchemy, as revealed by the Tarot trump. All the elements described by the oracle appear in the trump, which is a representation of taking material without life and raising it to higher levels. The overtones are spiritual, but they have their matches in the material world. The exchange of colours between the lion and eagle represent an advanced stage of balance and harmony. What the woman is creating in her cauldron is birth, growth and purification. Those who are familiar with the symbolism will see this reflected everywhere in the mystery of life. What it means in concrete terms is that the woman has succeeded. Material without life has been given life; circumstances once inert or uncertain are transformed into a desirable situation. It may be one of the most mystical of oracles, but it is among the most potent indicators of a fortunate outcome.

Conclusion

Sun in Sagittarius indicates a desire for an extension of Self. The star sign's corresponding Tarot card, trump XIV, means the joining of forces, harmonious partnerships, success. On the Tree of Life the sign and trump occupy a vital path on the middle pillar, between the spheres of Moon and Sun. The entry of Sun into the world of the Tarot character shows a goal accomplished, an objective won. It is a major step, terminating in a sphere central not only to the Tree, but to life itself. It is the air of Sun breathing new life into the fire of Sagittarius.

7 in 10

7= Venus, 10= the star sign Capricorn and Tarot trump XV, The Devil. Venus rules the element fire, Capricorn is of earth.

The Carver

The old man of the mountain is viewing his world anew. He is a true man of earth; practical, solid, not given to flights of fancy. He takes what he needs from the mountain to survive. But he has grown tired of his daily routines. He fells a tree and begins to carve.

Inspired by the high view he carves a work to admire, a work to keep for his pleasure. Hour by hour he carves and the day falls to twilight.

It has grown too dark to carve, and too dark to hunt or take from the mountain what he needs to survive. The old man of the mountain takes his work of art back to his rock-built home. Lighting a fire, he places upon it the work he has carved. Tonight he will stay warm. Tomorrow he will eat.

Summary

Sometimes what we think we want, and what we really need, does not coincide. The Tarot character here has everything he needs to hand. The mountain has served him well through the years, and he has learned how to turn its sparse offerings to his advantage. It may not be an easy life, or one filled with luxury, but it is a life in tune with his honest requirements. Turning his back on that, if only for a day, has taught him that viewing his world anew was a shallow act. Instead of attempting to branch out in a new direction, and occupy himself with unfamiliar works, he would have fared better going about his daily routines with, perhaps, a little more gratitude. To change what clearly does not need changing serves no practical purpose.

Conclusion

Venus in Capricorn indicates the desire to seek status through wealth and possessions. Capricorn's corresponding Tarot card, trump XV, The Devil, means ambition, blind impulse, secret activities. On the Tree of Life the sign and trump occupy the path between the spheres of Mercury and Sun. The entry of Venus is a slightly retrograde step. The upsurge of emotions is something that disturbs the Tarot character; it is unnatural for him to be anything other than creative energy in its lowest (material) form. He begins to experience feelings and sentiments that cloud his otherwise sharp and reliable vision. It is the fire of Venus consuming the earth of Capricorn.

8 in 11

8= Mercury, 11= the star sign Aquarius and Tarot trump XVII, The Star. Mercury rules the element water, Aquarius is of air.

Responding to Necessity

A cave in which water drips may display objects like teeth. From the roof they hang down, tapering to a point. From the ground they rise up, tapering to a point. They are forms to admire; they make the traveller pause and respect the labour of thousands of years.

Though simple in shape, their slow growth is beyond the grasp of mankind to emulate. They are visible tributes to nature's laws responding to necessity.

When flesh, blood, bone and sinew respond to necessity, the labour of thousands of years cannot be emulated. Yet what can be achieved in a single moment, are intelligent creations beyond the grasp of nature. Those who feel small in the world should learn not to fear a cave with teeth, no matter its age.

Summary

Responding to necessity is an oblique reference to processes or events taking a particular course of action because they must. They are the laws of chemistry and physics, which in turn are based entirely on nature. Put simply, some events have to happen as there is little other choice. That is the underlying theme of this oracle, in which stalagmites and stalactites are used to represent the slow but solid results of unseen natural laws.

Nature may have no choice for it has no free will, only natural selection. We, on the other hand, are free to make unnatural choices.

Our responses to what we see as a necessity may take any route we choose; we are not bound by natural law. It is exactly that freedom which allows us to apply our intelligence to any situation. The cave with teeth is a metaphor for something perceived as awesome and larger than life. It is daunting and enough to put anyone off their balance. But that balance should be recovered quickly, for with intelligence we are free to prove that size really is unimportant, and if we choose the correct response even a cave with teeth will fall before us.

Conclusion

Mercury in Aquarius indicates great individuality and a markedly intuitive nature. The star sign's corresponding Tarot card, trump XVII, The Star, means clearness of vision, unexpected help, new outlook. On the Tree of Life the sign and trump occupy a high path between the spheres of Sun and Neptune. The entry of lower-aspected Mercury into the world of the Tarot character is strictly speaking a backward step, but this is largely offset by Mercury's links with communication, as it is the function of The Star to inform the world with her spiritual light. It does, however, introduce an element of rationality that was previously absent. With rational thought comes doubt and circumspection, and Mercury soon becomes his trickster self. It is the water of Mercury misting the air of Aquarius.

9 in 12

9= Luna, 12= the star sign Pisces and Tarot trump XVIII, The Moon. Luna rules the element air, Pisces is of water.

The Shadows

One moon in the sky brings howling to dogs, tides to the oceans.

Two moons in the sky is a warning of hell hounds baying, of tides that rise to great heights to inflict their destruction.

Faced with the unthinkable, those who are free to go where they choose will retreat. Those who must stay should not stay alone; nor should they burden their friends. Let them approach those who are born to fight, prepared to fight, equipped to fight. Their enemy is not the moonlight, but the shadows.

Two moons will not defeat those who scorn baying hounds and rising waters. After moonlight, the sun rises.

Summary

The baying hell hounds and tides of destruction are simply warnings of extremely negative influences at work. The images are deliberately startling, for this is an oracle of the gravest caution. The hounds, tides and shadows are various threats that wait their moment. Specialist knowledge is the best way to deal with them, which does not have to be from paid professionals; it could be from anyone with helpful experience of escaping that particular situation. They at least will be the best placed to 'scorn baying hounds and rising waters'. No other oracle offers this level of warning, therefore it should be given the closest attention. The sun will rise only after the situation has been resolved. Unless, of course, swift retreat is possible beforehand.

Conclusion

Luna in Pisces indicates an over-active imagination, which may lead to health problems. The star sign's corresponding Tarot card, trump XVIII, The Moon, means deception, a crisis of faith, the brink. Luna entering the world of this trump effectively doubles the negative connotations. Gateways are opened which are best left firmly closed and untouched thereafter. It is the air of Luna and the water of Pisces joining in a black cloud.

Appendix
Meaning of Numbers in the Series 1 – 12

Star Signs and Tarot Cards

1   *Aries the Ram.* Aries is of the element fire, and indicates people who are bold, outgoing, inspirational and perceptive. In keeping with their fiery temperament they may lack subtlety and at times display aggression. The sign is ruled by Mars. The corresponding Tarot card, trump IV, The Emperor, shows a male figure seated so that his figure forms the alchemical symbol of sulphur, representing the male fiery energy of the universe. In divination the trump means conquest, victory, energy, stubbornness and ill-temper. The sign and trump occupy the 28th path, called the Natural Intelligence.

2   *Taurus the Bull.* Taurus is of the element earth, and indicates people who are loyal, sensitive, calm and affectionate. In keeping with their earthy temperament they can be firm, productive and generous. The sign is ruled by Venus. The corresponding Tarot card, trump V, The Hierophant, shows a male robed figure bearing a wand and surrounded by four Kerubs, guardians of the shrine. He is the Manifestor of the Mysteries, and his throne is a bull. In divination the trump means stubborn strength, toil, help from superiors, peace. The sign and trump occupy the 16th path, called the Eternal or Triumphal One.

3   *Gemini the Twins.* Gemini is of the element air, and indicates people who are cheerful, intelligent and highly adaptable. In keeping with their airy nature they can be cold and unemotional. The sign is ruled by Mercury. The corresponding Tarot card, trump VI, The Lovers, shows a young male and female standing before a

mysterious hooded figure. This figure is a form of Mercury, the god of communication, and also The Hermit of trump IX. The image shows the marriage or combining of opposites, in the quest to achieve perfect unity. In divination the trump means intelligence, swift adaptability, intuition and a tendency towards instability. The sign and trump occupy the 17th path, called the Disposing One.

4   *Cancer the Crab.* Cancer is of the element water, and indicates people who are considerate, impressionable, sensitive and with strong family ties. Like water, they may seek their own level without reference to others. Cancer is the house of the Moon; also Jupiter, the god of abundance, is exalted in Cancer. The corresponding Tarot card, trump VII, The Chariot, shows a male figure in armour. He is in a chariot drawn by four sphinxes composed of a bull, a lion, an eagle and a man. His purpose is to bear the Holy Grail and bring spiritual light in the darkness. In divination the trump means ruthlessness, obedience, victory, faithfulness, violence. The sign and trump occupy the 18th path, called the Intelligence of the House of Influence.

5   *Leo the Lion.* Leo is of the element fire, and indicates a person who is protective, confident, progressive and expressive. Their fiery nature can lead them to be lustful and egotistical. The sign is ruled by the Sun. The corresponding Tarot card, trump XI, Lust, shows a naked woman riding a lion with seven heads. The woman is an image of the Moon illuminated by the Sun, and the trump represents the reining of passions for spiritual purposes. In divination the trump means strength, resort to magick, energy and action, the opportunity to advance. The sign and trump occupy the 19th path, called the Intelligence of all the Activities of the Spiritual Being.

6   *Virgo the Virgin.* Virgo is of the element earth, and indicates a person who is precise and meticulous, helpful and dependable. In keeping with their earthy nature they can be secretive and totally dependent. The sign is ruled by Mercury. The corresponding Tarot card, trump IX, The Hermit, shows a cloaked figure bearing a lamp, the centre of which is the Sun.

The entire image is essentially that of fertility. In divination the trump means illumination from within, withdrawal and isolation, practical plans, secret impulses. The sign and trump occupy the 20th path, called the Intelligence of Will.

7   *Libra the Balances.* Libra is of the element air, and indicates a person who is refined, impartial, sociable and artistic. In keeping with their airy nature they can be indecisive and superficial. The sign is ruled by Venus. The corresponding Tarot card, trump VIII, Adjustment, shows a masked woman on toe-tip, crowned with the plumes of Maat, the Egyptian goddess of justice. From the plumes are suspended scales, balancing Alpha against Omega, the first against the last. She holds a great sword, again symbolizing justice. The image is that of obtaining balance from the whirling dance of creation. In divination the trump means marriage, partnerships, negotiations, the vindication of truth. The sign and trump occupy the 22nd path, called the Faithful Intelligence.

8   *Scorpio the Scorpion.* Scorpio is of the element water, and indicates a person who is creative, seductive, inspires faith and often drawn to the mysteries. Their watery nature can see them destructive and vengeful. The sign is ruled by Mars. The corresponding Tarot card, trump XIII, Death, shows a skeletal figure bearing a scythe. The skeleton and scythe are symbols of Saturn, a form of Chronos, the god of time famous for devouring his children, for in the end time consumes all. The image portrays the continuing elastic element in nature, in which nothing is eternally fixed. In divination the trump means change, transformation, starting afresh, destruction. The sign and trump occupy the 24th path, called the Imaginative Intelligence.

9   *Sagittarius the Archer.* Sagittarius is of the element fire, and indicates a person who is straightforward, generous, bold and intelligent. In keeping with their fiery nature they can be coarse and prone to gluttony. The sign is ruled by Jupiter. The corresponding Tarot card, trump XIV, Art, shows a predominately female figure with a combined male and female head; before her is a cauldron on a fire flanked by a white lion and a red eagle. The symbolism is again that of alchemy; the raising of inert material to spiritually-

informed life by the combination of opposites. In divination the trump means the way of escape, success after elaborate actions, control of volatile situations. The sign and trump occupy the 25th path, called the Intelligence of Probation, or Tentative One.

10 *Capricorn the Goat.* Capricorn is of the element earth, and indicates a person who is loyal, trustworthy, prudent and a good organizer. In keeping with their earthy nature they can be unsympathetic and demanding. The sign is ruled by Saturn. The corresponding Tarot card, trump XV, The Devil, shows a Himalayan goat with spiral horns and an eye in the centre of its forehead. This is a form of the Greek god Pan, the All-Begetter, who stands before a phallic tree which pierces the heavens. His approach can bring panic, for his name is the root of the word. The image represents the transcendence of all limitations. In divination the trump means ambition, blind impulse, unscrupulous methods, hidden forces at work. The sign and trump occupy the 26th path, called the Renovating Intelligence.

11 *Aquarius the Water-bearer.* Aquarius is of the element air, and indicates a person who is a social animal, loyal to a cause, and works towards brotherhood. Their airy nature can see them flighty and impractical. The sign is ruled by Uranus and Saturn. The corresponding Tarot card, trump XVII, The Star, shows a female figure holding two cups; one is raised aloft and the contents pour over her, the other is allowed to tip and spill upon the ground. The raised cup is gold and contains the ethereal water of life; the lowered cup is silver and contains the nectar of creation. The woman is the Great Mother, the goddess made manifest, imbuing the world with spiritual light and the inexhaustible possibilities of existence. In divination the trump means clearness of vision, the expansion of horizons, unexpected help, new outlook. The sign and trump occupy the 15th path, called the Constituting Intelligence.

12 *Pisces the Fishes.* Pisces is of the element water, and indicates a person who is imaginative, unselfish, creative and with strong spiritual aspirations. Their watery nature can see them attempting to control others. The sign is ruled by Neptune. The

corresponding Tarot card, trump XVIII, The Moon, shows two forbidding black towers with Anubis, the jackal god of Egypt, in double form guarding the way. Beneath them is a scarab beetle bearing the sun, as yet to turn night into day. The complete image represents the final decline into matter of all superior forms. In divination the trump means deception, illusion, hysteria, a crisis of faith, the brink. The sign and trump occupy the 29th path, called the Corporeal Intelligence.

Meaning of Numbers in the Series 3 – 9

The Planets

3. *Saturn.* Saturn occupies the third sphere, called Understanding. Saturn represents natural law, order and government; also restriction and decline in its negative aspects. In Greek mythology Saturn was known as Chronos, who became the god of time. His father was Ouranos, the earliest of the gods; his mother was Ge, the goddess of Earth. The name of Saturn is very closely linked with that of Satan, the tempter.

4. *Jupiter.* Jupiter occupies the fourth sphere, called Mercy. Jupiter represents stability, growth, maturity and magnificence. The Greeks knew Jupiter by the name of Zeus, the Olympian god who sat on his divine mountain with the staff of life in one hand and a thunderbolt in the other. He is very much a father-figure, presiding over the lesser gods and mankind, to whom he is guardian of the home.

5. *Mars.* Mars occupies the fifth sphere, called Strength. Mars represents energy, turbulence, cruelty, aggression and energetic expression. Known to the Romans as the god of war, and to the Scandinavians as the hammer-wielding Thor, to the Greeks he was the unpopular Ares. Ares had two sons, Deimos and Phobos, meaning Fear and Dread, which became the Greek names of the Martian moons.

6. *Sun.* Sun occupies the sixth sphere, called Beauty. Sun represents integration, balance, creative strength and harmony. Our Sun was seen by early man as the chief of all the gods, an obvious conclusion given its visual and physical dominance. This was a later modification of the woman as dominant goddess, when the

role of a man in producing a child was finally understood. Previously, it was thought that childbirth was something all females managed from start to finish magically and by themselves. Most cultures throughout recorded history have the Sun as their prime god; Ra to the Egyptians, Apollo to the Romans, Helios to the Greeks, Mithra to the Persians, and Hu to the Druids.

7. *Venus.* Venus occupies the seventh sphere, called Victory. Venus represents love and the lower associated emotions of desire, purely sensual pleasure, promiscuity etc., also sympathy and sexual polarity, the stirrings of Mother Nature. In ancient Greece Venus was known as Aphrodite Pandemos, signifying "Venus of all the people", for she granted social graces. One of her sacred symbols is the dove.

8. *Mercury.* Mercury occupies the eighth sphere, called Glory. Mercury represents the intellect, logical thought, cunning, trickery and communication. Mercury's staff, known as the caduceus, is topped by a pair of wings and entwined by two serpents, and is employed today as the emblem of the medical profession. Mercury's attribute of a teacher to the healing fraternity is of ancient origins, and has parallels in many cultures. He is above all a messenger of the gods, a communicator of divine knowledge.

9. *Luna.* Luna is our Moon, and it occupies the ninth sphere, called Foundation. Luna represents the subconscious mind, rhythmic change, fluctuation, receptivity. To the Romans she was Ceres, goddess of corn and wheat; to the Greeks she was Diana the huntress. She was also Vesta, goddess of the revered Vestal Virgins. A female deity throughout mythology, the Moon was frequently seen as consort to the Sun. It was, in every sense, a marriage made in heaven. The Vatican, or the "Mother Church", was chosen to be built on Mount Vaticanus, once a shrine to a female goddess.

List of Oracles

Number	Title	Page
3 in 1	Leadership	31
3 in 2	The Abyss	129
3 in 3	Firm Foundations	59
3 in 4	Unassailable	157
3 in 5	Beyond Reach	87
3 in 6	The Owl	185
3 in 7	Reunion	115
3 in 8	Stillness	45
3 in 9	Water and Rock	143
3 in 10	Fortunate Days	73
3 in 11	The Friendly Voice	171
3 in 12	Jackals	101
4 in 1	Careful Husbandry	103
4 in 2	Helping Hands	33
4 in 3	The First Gifts	131
4 in 4	Pleasure	61
4 in 5	Unbreakable	159
4 in 6	True Authority	89
4 in 7	Square and Circle	187
4 in 8	Cutting Down	117
4 in 9	United Effort	47
4 in 10	Denial	145
4 in 11	Abundance	75
4 in 12	The Net	173

5 in 1	Expertise	175
5 in 2	Two Friends	105
5 in 3	Discord	35
5 in 4	Providence	133
5 in 5	Turmoil	63
5 in 6	The Storm	161
5 in 7	Willing Acceptance	91
5 in 8	Talent and Aptitude	189
5 in 9	The Servant	119
5 in 10	Unrelenting Steps	49
5 in 11	The Cart	147
5 in 12	The Alley	77
6 in 1	Improvements	79
6 in 2	The Important Rose	177
6 in 3	New Ground	107
6 in 4	Consolidation	37
6 in 5	Marriage	135
6 in 6	The Open Door	65
6 in 7	The Confident Voice	163
6 in 8	Respite	93
6 in 9	Eagle and Lion	191
6 in 10	Spring	121
6 in 11	New Life	51
6 in 12	The Roadside	149
7 in 1	Bounds of Reason	151
7 in 2	Devotion	81
7 in 3	Two Trees	179
7 in 4	Remain Loyal	109

7 in 5	Union	39
7 in 6	The Pendulum	137
7 in 7	Cutting Through	67
7 in 8	The Iron Grip	165
7 in 9	The Cauldron	95
7 in 10	The Carver	193
7 in 11	Filling a Jug	123
7 in 12	Hidden Deeps	53
8 in 1	Haste	55
8 in 2	Management	153
8 in 3	Necessary Duty	83
8 in 4	Contingency	181
8 in 5	Shut and Open	111
8 in 6	The Silent Flower	41
8 in 7	Weighing Memories	139
8 in 8	Assessment	69
8 in 9	The Hinge	167
8 in 10	Begin the Ascent	97
8 in 11	Responding to Necessity	195
8 in 12	Brother and Sister	125
9 in 1	The New Road	127
9 in 2	Bolder Steps	57
9 in 3	Beginning and Preparing	155
9 in 4	Stealth	85
9 in 5	The Dwarf and the Giant	183
9 in 6	The Glow	113
9 in 7	End of Decrease	43
9 in 8	Making Entry	141

9 in 9	The Rainbow	71
9 in 10	Integrity	169
9 in 11	No Reward	99
9 in 12	The Shadows	197

CPSIA information can be obtained at www.ICGtesting.com
Printed in the USA
LVOW060939050412

276286LV00001B/36/P